God, Are You Listening?

God, Are You Listening?

· · · · · · ·

Free Yourself from
What Is Holding You Back

ELIZABETH HUTCHINSON

TURNING
STONE
PRESS

First published in 2012 by Turning Stone Press, an imprint of
Red Wheel/Weiser, LLC
With offices at:
665 Third Street, Suite 400
San Francisco, CA 94107
www.redwheelweiser.com

ISBN (paperback): 978-1-61852-004-3
ISBN (hardcover): 978-1-61852-003-6

Library of Congress Cataloging-in-Publication Data available
upon request

Cover design by Jim Warner

Printed in the United States of America
IBT
10 9 8 7 6 5 4 3 2

Contents

Gratitude

All glory for this book must be given to God. These are his teachings and I was fortunate enough be used as the transcriber.

I have had my prayers answered in so many ways. I have received assistance, support, and guidance from numerous individuals who have been instrumental in my growth and the creation of this book.

I must acknowledge the following individuals. My husband Bill provided much love and support during this entire writing process. My friends Jenny and Chantal gave feedback and encouragement. Delores provided a peaceful writing space on her property and I was able to be near nature every day. My nieces Kaitlyn and Megan and my nephew Joey provided insightful and thought-provoking questions as I shared my writing with them. My mother, Myrtle, gave her support and enthusiasm for this endeavor. Numerous family members, friends, and clients shared their experiences with me throughout the years, which provided the many examples used for the book and allowed me to experience incredible learning and love.

Author's Note

This is a nondenominational spiritual self-help book. It is intended for people of all faiths, religions, and belief systems, as well as nonbelievers. *God, Are You Listening?* is not about religion, although much of the content is phrased in religious terms. This book is about finding your spirit and maintaining the wondrous creation of you.

When I use the word *God* and the pronouns *He*, *His*, and *Him*, this does not mean that I see God as a man. Please feel free to change the word *God* to Buddha, Jesus, Holy Spirit, Creator, Mohammed, Jehovah, Beloved, Divine, Universe, Mother Earth, or whatever belief you have. I use the word *God* and the masculine pronouns throughout the book because I was raised with this terminology and find it comforting.

All the stories in the book are true, but the names and identifying information have been changed to protect privacy. Many of the stories are from women because the majority of my career was spent specializing in women's programs, but when working with men, the issues, thoughts, and feelings were similar. Often men find it discouraging when they can find stories about only women. The techniques in this book are suitable for everyone.

I used stories from my own life to describe my journey and the stories of others. The stories are my recollection and are recorded to the best of my ability. The techniques used in the book can be considered as a "toolbox" to address different aspects of the human state. For some the need is balance, for others the need may be freedom or forgiveness and/or acceptance; choose whatever technique you need. Each story and technique is a part of the journey to a deepening and transforming relationship with God. Mind-body-spirit connection helps to lead you to God with God. You are accepted wherever you are on our journey, and the process may take years. I used these techniques to help myself and others, and I hope that you will find comfort and support when you explore the material. The process is itself a journey. I encourage you to take the first step to deepening your relationship with God—you will not be disappointed.

God, Are You Listening?

Preface

Ahh . . . my beautiful bed. As I lie on the bed I start to feel the tension leave my body. I pray to God that I can have a full night's sleep. I cannot remember the last time I slept through the night. Another busy workday in the Victim Service office. I was in court with clients for a sexual-assault trial resulting in yet another acquittal. I returned to the office at five thirty p.m. to retrieve messages and return urgent calls. It was seven p.m. when I started to clean off my desk and a Royal Canadian Mounted Police (RCMP) member stopped to ask about a case. By the time we wrapped up it is pushing eight p.m.

I drag my tired body to the car for the short journey home. As I come through the door of my home I smell the aroma of food. As I round the corner into the kitchen I notice the single plate at the table and I realize I have missed yet another meal. My husband enters the kitchen and offers to heat my dinner; I let out a sigh and tell him, "I am too tired to eat." I enter the living room and sit in the big comfortable chair in front of the television, watching but not really seeing or hearing what is playing. It is a comedy, but I have no energy to laugh. Finally, I decide that I should eat and I make my way to the kitchen, I open the fridge and stare inside. I close the fridge empty-handed and decide to look in the pantry, but all the food looks like it needs preparation. I settle on toast because I think my empty stomach can handle it—after all, I have not eaten or had anything to drink all day. After more of my blankly staring at the television screen and sitting in a comatose state, my husband helps me out of the chair and guides me down the hallway to bed. I look at the clock and it brightly displays eleven p.m. Maybe tonight I will sleep uninterrupted.

I can hear a noise; is it a dream? No, it is coming from my bedside. Is it the alarm? I hit the alarm clock. It is 12:10 a.m., but it does not stop. My mind finally registers that it is the telephone. I quickly grab the telephone because I do not want my husband to wake up. I groggily say, "Hello." I hear a female voice informing me it is RCMP Dispatch and there was a motor-vehicle fatality and the RCMP requests my presence on scene. I struggle to wake and I silently slip out of bed to write the location of the incident and gather all pertinent information. I quickly splash some water on my face, run a brush through my hair, and get dressed. As I head out the door, I grab my Victim Service bag with all my essential resources.

As I approach the car I notice a light frost has begun to settle. I turn on the car and I let it warm up a bit before leaving. As I head out the driveway, I stop to ensure that I have my pants on because I cannot remember getting dressed—thankfully I do. I give my face a slap to wake up.

I start my conversation with God just like every other time I have attended a crisis call-out. I ask God to ensure the safety of the RCMP, paramedics, coroner and any other emergency personnel on scene. I pray for the family members who have lost a loved one and I pray for anyone who may have witnessed the crash. I ask for wisdom, guidance, and support as I work with the individuals connected to the crash. But tonight, I also pray that I remain awake to get to the scene and I do not cause a crash. I give myself another slap in the face to wake up and I roll down the car window to allow the cool night air to bring some freshness into the car and to hit my face.

As I drive down the road I wonder how much longer I can continue to function without sleep and I pray that I am attentive enough to clients that they do not notice the bags under my eyes. I drive approximately forty kilometers (twenty-five miles) in the dark through the fog, alert to animals that may cross my path. I start to see the flashing red and blue lights from the police cars up ahead. I am getting closer and reduce my speed. I say another prayer.

An RCMP member greets me and provides an overview of the situation. The family of the deceased lives in another community, and I thank God because I caught a break and it is not my job to attend the home to inform the next of kin that their loved one just died. I have a flash of guilt because I know one of my colleagues will be awakened to perform the next-of-kin notification with the RCMP.

Now I must focus on providing support to the witnesses of the car crash. I provide blankets and water, and put people in my car to warm up. I provide emotional support and ensure that everyone either has alternative transportation or is in a fit state of mind to drive. I say my goodbyes to the emergency staff and I return to the office to complete paperwork. (I could go home, but I am never able to fall back asleep.) After completing my paperwork I have a brief chat with the RCMP members. It is my way of leaving my work at the office. The clock now reads three a.m.

I enter my driveway and I see two deer munching on some grass nearby. Everything is serene and I wonder if I just dreamt the last few hours. I open the car door and a blast of cold air hits me and I know it was no dream. I quietly enter the house. I get undressed and return to bed. It is now 3:20 a.m. Well, I can get a few hours' sleep before going into work at eight a.m. I close my eyes, but I hear the telephone again. I pick it up and say, "Hello." I hear a male voice tell me it is RCMP Dispatch and I am required at the hospital due to a sexual assault. I drag my body out of bed and do the routine all over again. Thankfully the hospital is near my home.

I once again say some prayers. I am greeted at the hospital emergency-room door by the RCMP and provided with an overview. I enter the gynecology room with the RCMP member, who introduces me to the client. I stay with the client during the sexual-assault exam and provide emotional support. Once I have finished working with the client I return to the office to complete the paperwork. Once again, I know I cannot return home and immediately fall asleep. After a debriefing with the RCMP members I look at the clock, preparing to go home, and it now reads six a.m. I start for the door and I hear footsteps behind me. As I turn I see an RCMP member waving his hand, motioning for me to return. I am informed that there has been a sudden death and we are required at the residence.

I go to my car and I sigh, pushing all my tiredness deep down because I need to focus on the task ahead. I pray to God on behalf of the family, but I decide there is no point to pray for myself because there are just too many people in more distress than I am. Who am I to complain about being tired? I travel to the residence of the deceased and I provide emotional support to the family.

I decide this time I will go home, but not to sleep; I need to shower and change clothes because it is now seven thirty a.m. After a hot shower I feel better. I grab a bagel and an apple on my way out the door and I glance at the clock. It is 7:55 a.m. I will be able to get to work on time.

It is now twenty-four hours later, and I have worked with two different RCMP shifts and I begin to work with a third. I start returning messages left from the previous day. I meet with clients who have scheduled appointments or have dropped into the office unexpectedly. I make follow-up phone calls from the new intakes received overnight that did not require my immediate attention for a crisis call-out. I also contact families and professionals from the incidents I attended throughout the night. I agree to accompany the family of the deceased from the car-fatality incident to the morgue for a viewing scheduled for the following day.

A colleague stops by the office to say goodnight because it is now four p.m. and her shift has ended. We chat briefly about the number of call-outs, the workload, and how it is a typical day in the Victim Service office. I mention that I am tired and my colleague carries on. I work until the end of my shift at five p.m.

The RCMP members all wish me a good night and let me know they will do their best not to call me out tonight. I appreciate their support, but all of us know that the incidents are beyond our control. From moment to moment we never know what to expect. I approach my car and I start to pray for a quiet night, but I stop. . . . Why bother? Does prayer really work?

☙ 1 ❧

Unanswered Prayers

The Song of Moses
Deuteronomy 32:1–3 (New International Version)

Listen, O heavens, and I will speak;
Hear O earth, the words of my mouth.
Let my teaching fall like rain
and
my words descend like dew,
like showers on new grass,
like abundant rain on tender plants.
I will proclaim the name of the Lord.
Oh, praise the greatness of our God!

G OD, ARE YOU LISTENING? We have heard the old saying that prayers are always answered, but not always how we want it. Is that true? Some people believe prayers do not always get answered or are never answered.

It is easy to go to God with the big things like illness, death, etc., but it is the everyday things we forget about.

We believe we can handle or manage the day-to-day. Maybe it is because we think we should not bother God with the daily grind or maybe it is because we think we are supposed to be able to handle the small things ourselves, but whatever the reason, we fail to bring our struggles to God until it "really counts" and then we expect immediate attainment like Tinkerbell waving her magic wand.

When we encounter the big things in life we often reach out to God, even if we have proclaimed ourselves to be nonbelievers. During that time of crisis we bargain with God because, after all, we do not ask for much because we usually deal with things on our own; or we inform God we have been good Christian folk following his ways. Sometimes we rage at God because if He were just, how could He allow this horrific incident to occur, and while we rage, we expect miracles because, after all, Moses parted the seas, Jesus turned water into wine, and all we ask for is for God to remove an illness, repair a relationship, or bring someone back from the verge of death. We are not asking for much and in return we will do whatever is necessary to get our needs met. Even when God brings the loved one back from the brink of death or cures the illness, very few people praise God or remember the promises that were made during the cry for help—until the next crisis and the pattern repeats itself.

I have worked for more than eighteen years with people in crisis, and they tend to move from one crisis moment to the next. During that time of struggle they are willing to move mountains to change their circumstances, but usually within seventy-two hours, once the initial shock has worn off, they go back to the old ways of doing things; no longer is there an interest in making changes.

By the time we ask God for help, we have made such a mess out of our lives that much untangling must take place to rectify the matter. I am not saying that God does not perform instant miracles, because He does, but usually there is a need to start untying the knots and untangling the rope we have bound ourselves with. As God starts to untangle our mess, we decide that we no longer need God and we take our concern back and we "deal with it ourselves," and we slam God for not answering our prayers. The awesome thing about God is that He gave us Free Will and he allows us to take things back and create more knots and tangles. He does not ask for praise, but continues to show us loving kindness and engulfs us in love even though we have turned our backs on Him. He knows we will be back and He waits with wide-open arms to accept us in a loving embrace, just like healthy parents when their children leave home. And although parents know their children are not able to deal with all life situations on their own, they know it is time for their children to learn and grow, but they also know the door is always open and when their child is ready he will return home for the love that is needed to help repair whatever hurt the child has encountered.

Parents do not expect payment for loving and supporting their child and we know a child will very rarely ever utter the words, "You were right" to his parents. Children know coming home is the only answer and that they will not be turned away. I have witnessed some healthy families in action, but more often than not during my career and personal life I have encountered dysfunctional families. However, for the most part when a major crisis moment occurs, the family will step up and help—unless, of course, the family itself is the crisis. This example is like God, always waiting, always loving and ready to help, but we need to allow God to be there always in all ways.

It is easy to reach out and ask for help during an emergency. I have never encountered anyone at a car crash tell the emergency crews, "Go away and leave me alone; I will figure out how to get myself out of this car." And we do not tell the emergency crews, "She got herself into this car crash and now she can get herself out." Sometimes we are armchair specialists when rescue operations are happening, like when skiers go missing because they went out of bounds on a slope. We will watch the news and rant about the money it costs, the danger the rescue crews are being placed in, and say the idiots that disobey danger signs should be left to their own devices. But when it is us or our loved one who has gone out of bounds, we rage at everyone around us, demanding they do more to save us or our loved one. No one can do or does enough to help—not the police, doctors, nurses, teachers, friends, or family, and especially not God.

It is my belief that we have become a society that no longer looks to God for help, but expects others and material possessions to fix us. When we do look to the professionals for help and they do not provide an instant solution, we rant about the useless service our hard-earned tax dollars are paying for. We are loath to hear we need to do the work and maybe we need to look within and repair some of the damage, and while doing it reach out to a higher source for guidance and support.

As a professional working in the mental-health field, employed by or contracted by the government, I cannot mention God on the job, and if I do it must be in a passing comment like, "Do you belong to a faith group? If so, you may want to reconnect, and if not, is that something you've considered?" The government has just reasons and it is attempting to protect clients who are vulnerable. If you are self-employed in the mental-health field you can have sessions that speak openly about God, angels, and anything else that you may want to explore.

I provided psycho-educational information about self-esteem, assertiveness, boundaries, exploration of childhood beliefs. . . the list goes on and on, but I never asked the client to go deep within and discover who they are spiritually. For a number of years I facilitated psycho-educational material and I do believe that it is important, but that alone will not make you happier.

It is only when you look deep within that you discover the light or the spirit that was meant to shine brightly—that is God. When you develop a relationship within—with God—you can look out and really change the world around you. You will be joyous; you will have better boundaries, be more assertive and have higher self-esteem because you cannot have a deep meaningful relationship with God without having these characteristics. It is impossible.

The formula is *Love yourself/Love God = Love the world.*

How to Get There

Here is the really big question—How do you you get there? The path is not easy, but nor is it difficult. Sound confusing? Well, it really is not.

Looking within is just like cleaning house: it takes effort, but at the same time it really is not very strenuous. Typically, the issue about cleaning the house is a lack of motivation. If we waited to get motivated to clean the house, my guess is that it would never get cleaned. Eventually, we decide that we must get up and just begin and as we do the work becomes easier than we had imagined and before we know it the work is complete and it was virtually painless.

Just like cleaning house, when going within you must take *action*. It will never happen if we just wait for it, and like cleaning house we often put it off until the timing is right or company is coming. Ever notice how we can be on our best behavior when company arrives (that is, if we really enjoy the visitors), and once they are gone we fall back into old patterns? Why is that? It was not difficult while they were visiting and in fact it was often enjoyable to put our worries on the shelf, to laugh and forget about the day-to-day issues that usually bring us great annoyance. Is it because we are being our authentic self or is it because we want to project our best self? A by-product of going within is being authentic and projecting our best self, but here is the best part: it can stay longer than the company.

Now you may say, That is all well and good, but the house gets dirty again and it needs to be cleaned; and you are correct—it does and so do we. The willingness to look within is act one. The second act is doing it, and the third act is continuing to do it—three easy activities to resolve a lifetime of chaos. Now you may ask, If it is so easy why isn't everyone doing it and why are we living with war, famine, and family violence? And you know what? God asks the same question.

When we look at these activities, we can become overwhelmed very quickly, just like when we look around the house and see that it needs to be cleaned. When we start to clean we often decide to clean one room at a time so it does not seem like such a huge task. We may decide to clean the house a room at a time over a period of days, and once completed we take a moment to appreciate our handiwork and start all over again. Starting to see the pattern?

Now let's start cleaning. . . .

This is a story I have told many times. I remember first reading it in *Chicken Soup for the Soul: 101 Stories to Open the Heart and Rekindle the Spirit* written and compiled by Jack Canfield and Mark Victor Hansen. This particular story is about Jack Canfield's personal experience.

Near Bangkok there is a temple that houses a ten-and-a-half-foot, solid gold Buddha. A group of monks from a monastery had to relocate a clay Buddha from their temple to a new location to make room for a highway. When the clay Buddha was being lifted it started to crack and the rain began to fall. The head monk, who was concerned about the Buddha being damaged, decided to wait until the rain stopped. He covered it with a large tarp to protect it from the rain.

Later that night the head monk went to check on the Buddha. As he put his flashlight under the tarp the beam of light revealed something shiny. The monk got a hammer and chisel to chip away the clay. As he knocked off pieces of clay, the Buddha became brighter and brighter. Many hours later the monk stood face to face with a solid-gold Buddha.

Historians believe that several hundred years before the monks' discovery, the Burmese army was about to invade Thailand. The monks covered the golden Buddha with clay in order to keep it from being taken by the army. It appears that all the monks were killed and the golden Buddha remained a secret until that historic day.

I remember that Jack Canfield's realization from the story was that we are all like the clay Buddha. We are covered in a layer of hardness created out of fear, but underneath it we have a 'golden Buddha', a 'golden Christ' or a 'golden essence' waiting to be discovered. Our golden essence or spirit got covered up and like the monk our job is to uncover it.

The journey of self-discovery is like mining for a hidden treasure and when we uncover our extraordinary precious gift of the spirit we are in awe of the splendor, just like the tourists that visit the temple. This story had tremendous impact on me and over the years I have read and retold this story many times. When I was working as a Life Skills Management Leader with groups of abused women, this story was often the stimulus for lessons on building self-esteem. As a gentle reminder to the women throughout the duration of the course, I would remind them of that Golden Buddha shining inside.

The Power of Words

"Whatever words we utter should be chosen with care for people will hear them and be influenced by them for good or ill."

—Buddha

Words are very powerful; they can inspire a nation to challenge injustice; they can make us laugh hysterically or cry uncontrollably. When working with victims of domestic violence and hearing their stories, I was told countless times that the bruises and bones heal, but the verbal onslaught is an open wound that runs deep for a very long time, much longer than the bruises and broken bones. Think of how quickly a bruise will begin to change color and fade; the whole process is usually over within a week or two. Broken bones may take months to heal. And words remain longer and the wounds are deeper. Why?

Bruises and bones are physical and visible, whereas words are spoken in the air, and we cannot see them. Contrary to the old childhood rhyme "Sticks and stones can break my bones, but words can never hurt me," anyone who has felt the sting of harsh words knows that words can be very painful. In criminal court, the system looks for physical and financial evidence because it is tangible. It is very difficult to prove a crime of verbal abuse. If a person has received a death threat, a case may be made, but again many hurdles will have to be overcome. In a case of verbal abuse it is very difficult to obtain charge approval and to get a conviction. But when speaking with victims, it is clear that verbal abuse is often the most damaging.

What is the difference between words that we can allow to slide off our back and words that penetrate deeply?

It can depend on the tone of voice, the language used, and what type of relationship we have with the person using the words. If a stranger calls you stupid while walking down the street, you may ignore the person. (or you could believe the stranger and think, Wow, even a stranger passing by can see that I am stupid). But if your spouse or parent calls you stupid, you may hurt for days or years.

Very early in my career, I was working every Friday with a group of women who were still living with an abusive spouse. From Monday to Thursday another facilitator focused on the cycle of violence and because I facilitated on Friday, I did not want to focus on violence with the weekend fast approaching; I wanted the women to have an opportunity to fully absorb the material and debrief the information before spending the weekend with their abusive partners.

I had discovered a gem at the library, a videotape called *Self-Esteem & Peak Performance* by Jack Canfield. I watched the video and I was inspired. I thought his message was clear and easy to understand, and there were simple steps that created immediate results.

When I had the opportunity to facilitate that Friday, I knew immediately that the videos would be an ideal component in my curriculum. I informed my coordinator of my plan and was told that it was a mistake because there was no way the group would be able to stay awake to watch a video at the end of the week, but she had not seen Jack Canfield in action.

I reached a compromise with the coordinator and she gave me permission to show the video in segments over several Fridays. The first day I presented the material the ladies did not want me shut the video off; they were hooked. I stopped the video every time Canfield suggested an activity. For example, in the muscle-testing activity one person holds out their arm, saying something that is true, like "My name is Elizabeth," and the other person tries to lower the arm. The person talking must try to resist the arm being lowered, and the arm will remain locked in place because the statement is true. Then you do the same action but say something that is not true, "My name is Fido," and again you resist, but the arm will easily lower, thus demonstrating the impact of our thoughts on our consciousness.

Each time I facilitated the group, I would caution the women to be careful about their new skills when interacting with their spouse, because I was concerned that their partners would see the changes occurring and hurt or kill them. I explained that because they were in tune with their partners, any change would be easily recognized and their partners may feel threatened and lash out. Safety planning was a major component of the curriculum each week. This information pertains to anyone in abusive relationships, men included. Many men experience violence, but it is not always acknowledged.

I often shared the national-average figure for people leaving abusive relationships, but would multiply it by one hundred to account for how many times they left mentally. Often people judge victims as being passive and not doing anything to stand up for themselves, but that is not true. Every time a person is verbally abused and they think that the other person was wrong or they think about how the abusive person was behaving and that they are projecting their actions onto the victim, they are fighting back.

One Monday morning, I was asked to join the women's group because something big had happened over the weekend, but I was not provided with any details. The fear was lodged in my throat and my colon because I assumed the worst had happened: one of the ladies had been seriously hurt after our Friday session and it was my fault. The women were sitting in their usual fashion, in a circle, and as I entered the room it became very quiet and my insides were twisting like a Philadelphia pretzel. I was trying to quickly count the participants to determine who was missing. A participant by the name of Eleanor stood up and asked me to sit in the circle. She asked me if I knew why I was asked to meet with them, and I replied no. Eleanor continued to talk and she said she had "really big news."

Eleanor proceeded to tell me that after she left group on Friday, she went home and her husband was in a mood, and she knew that she was in for a rough weekend. As he verbally abused her throughout the weekend, she continued to repeat silently, "I am worthy, I am lovable, I am worthy, I am lovable, I am worthy, I am lovable" to herself. She said that partway through the weekend he finally stopped, but the difference was inside her. She felt different, she was not exhausted, she was able to hold her head up high today, and she felt good inside. Eleanor told us it had been a long time since she had felt that good, and she compared her feelings to a time when she'd had a job she loved. Eleanor said the phrase saved her life and she was leaving the abuser. During the remainder of the program, Eleanor left her partner, her beliefs about herself continued to change, and she returned to the job she loved. I saw her a few times over the years and learned that she bought a house, she continues to do work that she loves, and to the best of my knowledge she has never entered another abusive relationship.

You never know what will impact someone; thus it is so very important to live your life with love because one small word, sentence, act, or smile, can actually save another. I am confident that Jack Canfield has no idea that when he developed the material for *Self-Esteem & Peak Performance* it would become a life preserver.

During the years following the Eleanor incident, I always used his material in my courses, and I added *Chicken Soup for the Soul* by Jack Canfield and Mark Victor Hansen. We would read a story from one of the books each morning before we started the day's lessons. We would randomly open a book because we believed whatever story we were supposed to hear for the day would be presented to us. We would discuss the story after each reading and I was always impressed by how someone would tell us how the story was exactly what they needed to hear that day and why it had such a profound effect on them.

Eleanor's story illustrates that words do matter, but the difference is the significance we give to them or choose not to give to them. Eleanor had been abused numerous times in the past by her partner, and her self-worth was extremely low because at some level she believed he was right. Each time he told her she was useless and worthless, she believed it. Eleanor would fight back mentally and sometimes think he was wrong, but she was unable to replace his words with anything new. She started to believe he was right and the belief was one of the reasons she remained trapped in the abuse. Not only was he abusing her, but she also was abusing herself. Each time Eleanor replayed those scenes in her mind, she was reinforcing the message that she was useless and worthless. It was only when she was able to replace the negative message with a new one of her own that her self-esteem began to rise.

When we attach to words spoken by others or the messages we give ourselves, we create our reality. The reason muscle testing is accurate is because it works like a computer exploring our files in our mind-body-spirit, and once it reads the information it produces the data we hold to be true. If the data has been entered incorrectly it has no way to determine if the information is false until we eliminate the information and enter new information. In Eleanor's case, she was entering new information, which resulted in a different outcome. Each of us has the power and capability to change our program and sometimes we will see immediate results and other times it will take repeated attempts to have the new information stick. It's not unlike when you start a new job: at first it is difficult to retain all the new information. As you repeat the tasks it gets easier and soon what was once new becomes familiar.

There is a lot of material out there about positive affirmations, and affirmations are very important, but the key is to ensure that you are fully connecting with the affirmation on all levels: mind-body-spirit.

What is spirit? The core of the earth always has a glow from the heat; now imagine it being in the central part of you that is your spirit or imagine a candle within the core of your being: it always has a flame, and it can be shining brightly or be very dim—it all depends on you and what you put in front of the flame to hide its glow.

Explore what words impact you, and when you hear certain words or phrases, what does your mind think? Is your mind agreeing or disagreeing or is your mind adding to the statement? You will also reject positive words if you do not believe the information to be true. Someone tells you that you look beautiful today and your mind thinks, What is wrong with your eyes? I feel fat and ugly.

I facilitated life skills/employment programs every day for eight years, and the groups varied in length and the number of participants. I facilitated groups with men and women wanting to overcome barriers to employment, and for a number of years I specialized in working with groups of abused women. Approximately halfway through the life-skills portion of the program, I facilitated an exercise on self-esteem. By this time the participants had spent numerous hours together and knew each other quite well. This was one of the many exercises used in this portion of the program: Each person in the circle has an opportunity to participate as a recipient and the recipient must remain silent unless needing clarification about a comment. The group shares what they like about the recipient. Often comments include the facts that the recipient is kind, has a great sense of humor, shares great insights, etc. A group recorder documents all the comments because often the recipient will forget or not hear (block) some of the statements. Once the exercise is completed the paper is given to the recipient as a reminder of all the positive qualities others see and appreciate. The recipient can only say "thank you" at the end of the session because the tendency is to discount some of the comments with explanations, sarcasm, or humor.

When a woman named Deanna participated in this exercise, she could not control her laughter and I asked her to explain to the group what was happening for her. She expressed that it was such a new experience to hear positive comments that it was difficult for her to absorb. She had a hard time remaining quiet and wanted to continually discount the comments. Eventually, she settled on laughter. Deanna described it as system overload. It was very sad to hear to that someone would be so unaccustomed to positive comments. The sound of her laughter was not joyous, but was clearly a coping mechanism to reject what was being presented to her. Deanna was very reluctant to explore her low self-worth, and she struggled for the entire program to allow her golden essence to shine; she did make progress, and allowed it to flicker.

What is your body telling you? When you are getting ready to present your proposal to the chairman of the board or present your paper to the class, what response are you receiving in your body? Is your stomach turning in knots? Is your heart racing? *Now check your mind and see what messages you are getting.* Are you telling yourself that everyone will dislike your ideas, you will be a laughing stock, you will die of embarrassment? Are you hearing your parents' words that you have no original ideas or are you telling yourself that your ideas will be so well-received that you will be promoted or the class will want copies of your paper?

When Ralph, a participant in another group during the self-esteem exercise, started to hear the positive comments, his knees began to quiver and then his whole body began to shake uncontrollably, and he started to make small moaning noises. I went to Ralph and put my hands on his shoulders and the shaking slowed and finally quit, along with the noises. When the group finished providing the positive feedback, they asked what had happened. I asked Ralph if he was willing to share his experience. Ralph stated that he was not used to hearing anything positive, he became overwhelmed, and he could not control his body. I explained to the group that although appreciative words were being given to Ralph, his mind and body were not accustomed to it and it was reacting to new data being entered. This was a classic example of mind-body connection. Ralph was very appreciative of the experience and he beamed all day, and he was able to hear positive comments from that day forward. Ralph's golden essence began to shine.

Are you starting to see the mind-body connection? You choose your feelings based on your thoughts and you act according to your beliefs and experiences. Replace the messages playing in your mind; view them as a broken compact disc, and replace the messages with a new compact disc. Once you start to have mind-body connection, you start to chisel the mud that has been corroding your system for years and your spirit starts to shine. This small change will allow your sprit to flicker, but sometimes it takes a lot of chiseling to see the glow.

Can you find that golden essence within? Eleanor found the Golden Buddha within and her life changed. She is alive, mind-body-spirit, now it is your opportunity.

Chapter Review:

- Observe your mind and the messages you are receiving.

- Observe your body's responses to the messages you are receiving.

- Explore mind-body connection.

- Read positive quotes and/or short stories upon getting up in the morning and before going to bed.

- Insert new data, change the CD.

- Look within and see your spirit/essence flicker, shine, or glow.

- Find a box or container and create a toolbox. Place a quote or inspiring book in the box. It is helpful to record your observations of opportunities for reflection. This book provides techniques and tools for making a change. Place each new tool in your toolbox to be used whenever you need.

**Journal pages have been provided at the back of the book because it is helpful to record your observations and use this as an opportunity for reflection.*

Embracing the Gifts God Gave Us

"YOUR JOKES ARE DOING ABSOLUTELY NOTHING FOR MY ENDORPHINS!"

www.CartoonStock.com

If you want to know the secret of good health, set up home in your own body, and start loving yourself when there."
—From the book *Simply Well,* by John W. Travis, MD, and Regina Sara Ryan

GOD EQUIPPED US WITH the most amazing gift that never seems to get acknowledged or celebrated; the gift is endorphins!

Endorphins are hormones that are produced in your brain and released in your bloodstream. Endorphins have been shown to control continual pain and feelings of stress and frustration. Endorphins are produced by a wide range of natural sources and free activities, such as exercise, food, nature, water, pets, music, laughter, intimacy and sex, therapeutic healing, sleep and rest, and deep breathing. Studies have shown that chronic stress, anger, and depression cause the body to create chemicals that can interrupt or stop the healing process and shorten life expectancy, while joy protects us from stress, illness, and premature death.

It is also important to understand your body and the messages that it contains. When you learn to listen to your body when it is in pain, and understand the messages it tries to tell you, you can then heal your mind-body-soul. This is important because then you can begin to learn to use the gifts that God gave you to improve your health.

Medical research on endorphins proves that a healthy mind-body-spirit is an essential life-giving force. The mind-body-spirit connection is obvious because we have the ability to make these wonderful little hormones!

Released endorphins can heal your mind-body-spirit in the following ways:

- Change your mood to feel positive and happy

- Improve your immune system

- Help to fight infection and viruses

It is time to release some endorphins to improve your mind-body-spirit connection.

Often we get caught up in the busyness of life and we become estranged from the center of our being. God is

intimately involved with human life. Our role is to preserve the gift of life until the time for the touch of the
Master's hand. Try embracing the gifts that God gave you
to help reconnect your mind-body-spirit.

Balance

"A journey of a thousand miles must begin with a single step."
— Lao-tzu, mystic philosopher

In any endeavor in life, balance is essential. When we start
out on a new journey for health we must be careful not to
turn it into a compulsive behavior. If you have not been
exercising or your activities have been limited, walking
eight kilometers (five miles) on the first day is not helpful
to your mind-body-spirit. There is no order of importance
with the techniques described in this chapter and I encourage you to pick one activity that appeals to you and con-
centrate on it for a time and then continue to add more
techniques as you become comfortable.

Be cautious that you do not develop unhealthy behaviors all in the name of better health. If you take any of the
techniques to the extreme and give the majority of your time
and attention to it and lose sight of others and your surroundings, you lose the intent of mind-body-spirit connection. On
the other hand, you may be thinking, *How can I balance my
already busy life with new techniques?* These techniques or tools
will not be demanding or conflict with your life unless you
believe them to be. They actually link together—you must
act for the essential purpose to heal your mind-body-spirit.

Exercise

"Lack of activity destroys the good condition of every human being, while movement and methodical physical exercise save it and preserve it."

—Plato

I can almost hear the groans from some of you as you read the title—*Exercise*—*yuck!* I completely understand if you are reacting this way because exercise was like a dirty word to me for a very long time. When I facilitated, I would bring in guest presenters for components that I was not mastering because if I was not trying to live it, I could not teach it. I could intellectually understand the point of exercise, but I lacked motivation and never seemed to remain consistent.

As it turns out, exercise does not need to be complicated and it too relates to the messages we give ourselves. I could tell myself that I just needed to get up and do it, but the overriding message I gave myself was that self-care was not a worthy endeavor or that I was being selfish. Basically, the message I received growing up was if you took time for yourself, including time to exercise, it was selfish and you were being lazy. If I wanted to walk there needed to be a goal attached and it could not just be for the health of it—the goal had to be work-related. Years later, even though I knew intellectually the importance of exercise for health, I continued to carry this message deep within, never identifying the mind-body-spirit connection.

In 2009, as my father lay dying in the hospital and as I watched him in the last hours of his life, I thought about why he was there. He had diabetes, heart disease, asthma, and arthritis. He'd had several heart surgeries, but he was a stubborn man and, although he suffered from these health issues, refused to follow doctors' instructions. He always stated no doctor was going to tell him what to do; he would eat what he wanted and he would continue to smoke. He was a meat-and-potatoes man and he always had to have his meat fried. He would load up on sweets and take more insulin to counteract the effects of not eating properly. His exercise regimen was limited and his smoking never slowed. He spent years taking a handful of medication morning, noon, and night. As I watched him labor for breath, I was disappointed he had chosen to treat his body in this manner; he had his first heart attack at the age of forty-five. At age seventy-one his mind was still razor-sharp, but he was dying because he refused to take care of his body. Then it hit me like a lightning bolt as I watched him dying and judged him for the way he treated his body after his diagnoses: I was no better. I was overweight, I did not exercise. The only differences were that I did not smoke and did not have any health problems (yet). I was forty years old and could prevent heart disease by making some lifestyle changes. Why wait until a heart attack to create change? It was at that moment I vowed my life would be different.

You do not need to run out and buy a membership to a gym to have better physical health; the simplest and easiest solution is walking. Like cleaning the house, you just need to do it and after you are finished, you will have a satisfied feeling because those endorphins are pumping.

Walking reduces your risk of heart disease by thirty to forty percent, and of diabetes and stroke by fifty percent—just walking thirty to sixty minutes per day. It is important to have a good pair of walking shoes because it affects your ankles, your knees, and your whole body. From my experience if you hurt, you quit and a good pair of walking shoes is a small price to pay to be able to live longer, to watch your children grow, to walk your daughter down the aisle at her wedding, or to enjoy retirement.

My friend Charles's father retired at the age of sixty-five from driving a logging truck and upon his retirement he decided that his new job was to sit in his easy chair, to watch TV, and to watch the world. His identity was wrapped up in his job as a truck driver and he could not envision himself as anything else. He had a wife, grown children, and many grandchildren, and he loved them dearly, but when his life changed and he no longer was in the role of the provider, he had no idea where he belonged and therefore decided the easy chair was his reward for years of backbreaking hard work. As the years progressed his health rapidly deteriorated and he started to complain that his retirement had become a full-time job of going to medical appointments. But as soon as the appointments were completed he returned to the chair. The last five years of his life he was barely able to move. He relied on his wife to help him out of the chair and to go to and from the bedroom or bathroom; he died in 2010.

When his father died, it was a huge wake-up call for Charles. He too was a truck driver and he noticed his weight gain, plus he was not getting any exercise. As Charles drove his truck, he would often be reaching into the lunch box to see what was available, and the highlight of his week was when his trucking route took him near the local meat shop so he could stop for some of his favorite sausage. Charles realized he was becoming his father, but long before retirement. He was not getting any physical exercise, and he continued to gain weight, plus he was starting to lack the motivation to move when he was not working. During this time of self-awareness, he was on a break from driving his truck and he started walking. He said the neighbors thought he was losing his mind because he was out walking in the early morning and it was such an unusual occurrence for him. Charles would walk at least two kilometers (one and a quarter miles) per day and got home in time to see the children off to school. He had the rest of the day to accomplish tasks that needed attention around the house and garage. Charles continued his exercise routine and became more aware of his eating habits. He lost weight and his overall mental, emotional, and physical well-being improved. He beams with delight at his new physical appearance and his spirit shines. Charles commented, "If Dad could have recognized the benefit of being active, he would be alive today to be able to provide guidance and support not only to me, but also to his many grandchildren that adored him."

Food

"The body needs material food every day. The soul needs spiritual food."

—Remez Sasson, author, creator, and owner of
www.SuccessConsciousness.com

Eating chilies and spicy food will also increase your endorphins! Try adding some jalapeños and chilies to your dishes. Proper nutrition fights symptoms of depression and helps to prevent many diseases. Give some consideration to how your food choices impact your health. Research which foods and cooking methods are the healthiest for you and take more control over your life to gain the best from it.

After my father's death I changed many things about my life, and one was food. I eat mostly vegan. I still indulge in eating fish, but I quit eating shellfish (because I made friends with a lobster and as I put him in the pot, I felt very guilty). I am not suggesting that you need to eliminate meat and dairy from your diet. However, I will encourage you to try eating no meat or dairy one day a week, just to see how you feel. Vegan eating has increased my energy level, decreased my allergies, and created the best bowel movements ever. If you decide to change to vegan cooking, I encourage you meet with a vegan to discuss cooking tips or take a class, because if tofu and other soy products are new to your menu, it is important to know how to prepare them properly. When I changed my diet I was surprised to learn how many items are soy-based, and grocery-shopping became an adventure because I needed to learn a completely new section of the store. Trying new recipes is an excellent way to introduce spices and chilies into your diet. At first the change may seem very time-consuming, but you will soon discover the rewards are well worth the effort.

T. Colin Campbell PhD and Thomas M. Campbell II, in their book *The China Study,* provide a comprehensive appraisal of nutrition and long-term health. Basically, I encourage you to be aware of what you are putting in your body and why. A young girl I know told her family that she volunteered to be the stage manager for a school play and her siblings responded with jibes about her usual inability to speak in front of groups (they were not trying to be mean, but were simply engaging in common sibling torment). Her mother was shocked that she would take on such a huge responsibility and expressed her concern that the child was in over her head. I watched the child stuff candy in her mouth as the comments were made and at times she had so many candies in her mouth, she was unable to talk. I observed her body being tense and her shoulders slouched, but she never verbally expressed her pain. As I gently took the candy jar from her and I commented on her courage to take a risk and how proud I was to see her step out of her comfort zone, her body began to relax and she stopped putting candy in her mouth. Often food is used as a coping mechanism for emotional pain. Be aware of why you are eating.

I attended the Celebrate Your Life Conference in Chicago in 2011, and Marianne Williamson, author of *A Course in Weight Loss: 21 Spiritual Lessons for Surrendering Your Weight Forever*, was one of the keynote speakers. She described the care we take to remove our nylons so there are no tears in them and to remove our dresses to ensure we don't get deodorant on them, and asked, Why do we not take the same or better care of the vessel we were given that covers our cells and bones? Marianne Williamson is completely correct. God gave us our body as a gift, but if we do not treasure it, it will wear out prematurely, just like our car. Medical science has made and continues to make great strides to replace our worn parts, but if we fill up our bodies with the spirit, the natural by-product is better health.

Nature

"The old Lakota was wise. He knew that a man's heart away from Nature becomes hard; he knew that lack of respect for growing, living things soon led to lack of respect for humans too. So he kept his youth close to its softening influence."
—Chief Luther Standing Bear, Lakota Sioux

"Even though we represent many different First Nations cultures and traditions, we all agree on one basic teaching. We were put here by the Creator to care for this land we call Mother Earth. This means we have a responsibility to maintain good relations with all of her creation."
—Assembly of First Nations, 1993

How much of your day, each day, is spent outdoors? For many the answer will amount to minutes. We leave our homes, we get into our cars, we drive to work or run errands, and at the end of the day we come back home. Some people get outdoors when the warmer temperatures come, but our bodies need fresh air more than seasonally. High oxygen levels increase the effectiveness of almost all the reactions in our bodies; our skin benefits, our lungs benefit, every system in our bodies benefit! Being in nature can lessen depression, and spending time in the sun will improve your mood. Some people are prone to depression due to a lack of sunlight (the disorder is called seasonal depression or Seasonal Affective Disorder—SAD).

When instructing about stress-management techniques, I use recordings of the sounds of the ocean, birds, or rain, which everyone finds quite soothing. Some people are concerned about subliminal messages in these tools; if you have this concern, I encourage you to spend some time in nature and record the sounds to be enjoyed at your leisure.

The First Nations always knew that there was a direct link between nature and spirituality, and we could learn from their teachings. When you open your heart, your eyes open too and you start to notice the flowers, trees, animals, and insects. You gain an appreciation for the work they do on earth; even the most minuscule plant or insect has a very important ecological role to play in the earth cycle. When the cycle is disturbed, we face long-term impacts.

One day a friend and I were having tea and discussing nature and I explained that I do not purposely kill mosquitoes, and she asked, What good are mosquitoes? She saw them as simply bloodsuckers, and a major annoyance. I stated I did not have a scientific answer, but I knew that they were food for fish and birds, etc., but I believed they must have another purpose or they would not have been created. The next time I turned on my computer, I Googled "mosquitoes" and this is the answer I discovered: Mosquitoes are nutrient-packed snacks for fish and other marine animals. They are also nutritious meals for birds, bats, and spiders. Their extinction, were it even possible, would have a huge adverse effect on the entire ecosystem. Huh.

How we treat the planet is vital to our survival. I am very impressed with young people, and the awareness and concern they have for the planet. They appear much more conscious of the consequences their actions have on the planet. When my teenage nephew is on a class break at school, he and his friends often wander to the community's downtown core to purchase snacks. When he is finished with his treat, if the container is recyclable and a bin is not available, he will carry the container back to school to place it in a recycle bin. It is very refreshing to know there is an understanding of the necessity to create change and to fix the problems that Generation X and the generations before us created.

Many indigenous cultures believe the land provides and sustains life, and having respect for the land and all its forms of life is pivotal in all customs, values, and spiritual beliefs. Learning and understanding the land and how everything is interconnected it is a part of spirituality. When you take off your shoes and allow your toes to feel the ground beneath you, you have a feeling of connectedness with something larger than yourself. The earth is good for the skin, and for many decades foot massages and spa treatments were unnecessary because the rocks from the earth naturally massaged the feet as people went about their daily routine. Mud baths were provided free of charge every time it rained. As children we often removed our shoes to feel the grass beneath our feet and we laughed with glee as the blades of grass tickled our feet. Do you remember sitting or lying on the earth, star-gazing or watching the clouds float by? Each time I throw away my adult cares about my clothing getting dirty or my concern that I might catch a cold, I envision the complete joy of being one with the earth. The indigenous people believe in a kinship with all creatures of the earth, sky, and water and call the animal kingdom "friend." They have always known the value of oneness with the earth and all its creatures and for many years other cultures tried to tell them differently. It is time we look to such cultures to understand and ask them to lead the way to help us move toward a stronger future.

We take for granted the fact that nature was made for us and we were made for nature. We have no right to this easy and casual belief. The movie *Avatar* was a wonderful image of human destructiveness. If we do not change our attitude we will continue to do what we have been doing all along with devastating results. When or if we discover how to live on other planets we will just repeat our patterns if we do not change our ways. But like in the movie, when we change our viewpoint we appreciate the bounty and beauty before us. I invite you to view all sources of life with graciousness and generosity.

Water

"We never know the worth of water till the well is dry."
—Thomas Fuller, *Gnomologia*

The inhabitants of the Western world take the value of water for granted. We are extremely blessed to have clean drinking water, and the ability to have running water, not only to cook with, but also to take long luxurious showers and soaks in the tub. I saw a poster recently stating earth should be called water because it is seventy percent water. Our bodies are seventy percent water and it is vital to life. Water is often overlooked as a stress reliever; every part of our body is dependent on water for healthy functioning. Normal daily activity causes the loss of about two liters (8 cups) of water, which must be replaced throughout the day. It can be quite dangerous to rely on thirst alone in determining your body's need for water; if you feel thirsty, you are probably already dehydrated. When we lack water it stresses our physical systems and we no longer work efficiently on all levels.

I used to think I drank a lot of water, but I realized that by the end of a workday that was often twelve to fifteen hours long, I had not consumed any water, and when I got home I drank glass after glass, but I was already very dehydrated. Start your day by drinking 500 milliliters (two cups) of water as soon as you get out of bed in the morning. Ensure that the water is room temperature or it may give you stomach cramps. At first it may be difficult to consume the water, but if you keep at it for one week, you will be able to continue the practice. Once I incorporated this routine into my life, I started to drink more throughout the day and by the end of the day I was no longer dehydrated, and my complexion improved, as did my overall health. If you are still struggling with the concept of drinking water, think about God, Buddha, or Jesus giving you a special present, which is your body or vessel, and the only maintenance required is proper hydration.

Dr. Masaru Emoto's book *The Hidden Messages in Water* describes how water is deeply connected to people's individual and collective consciousness. He explains the ability of water to absorb and hold human feelings and emotions. Using high-speed photography, he found that crystals formed in frozen water changed when focused thoughts were directed toward it. He found that water exposed to loving words showed brilliant, complex, and colorful snowflake patterns, while water exposed to negative words formed incomplete irregular patterns with dull colors. Dr. Emoto's crystal research demonstrated how the thought of failure changed the crystals, and because every part of our body is composed of water, he concluded that emotions affect our health in the same manner.

Dr. Emoto believes that since people are seventy percent water and the Earth is seventy percent water, we can heal our planet and ourselves by consciously expressing love and gratitude. Although immediate results are invisible to the human eye, they are there. Dr. Masaru Emoto believes when we love our body, it responds; when we send our love to the universe, it responds. Water is a great contributor to happiness and good health.

When working with people in trauma and crisis, I provided water as an essential element of aid because emotions would often get lodged in the throat, and the water lubricated the vocal cords to allow the individual to speak, it helped with fatigue, it helped cleanse the system of toxins, and it was important to keep the person hydrated since their level of stress was elevated due to the traumatic event.

Is it selfish or selfless to take a bath for relaxation? Many people, especially mothers, tell me that they cannot fathom taking a luxurious soak in the tub, and it has nothing to do with water conservation, it is because they believe it to be a selfish act. How can they take time to soak in a tub when laundry needs to be done, school lunches need to be made—besides, by the time they get the children to bed, they are too exhausted. By not taking responsibility for your health, which includes mind-body-spirit, you are not modeling holistic health for your children. When you are happier, you project happiness and have more energy to take care of the daily chores, and everyone benefits from a healthier and happier you.

In early times, herbal baths were used to help the sick while mineral baths were used for detoxification. The act of bathing stimulates blood circulation and calms the nervous system. It can also help relieve aches and pains, menstrual cramps, inflammation, and hemorrhoids. In our busyness, it is easy to forget to take care of ourselves, and a simple bath can help us to relax and be conscious each day. Create your own spa in your bathroom by lighting some candles and inform your household you are not to be disturbed. Do yourself and others a favor—take care of yourself!

Pets

"Animals are such agreeable friends—they ask no questions, they pass no criticisms."

—George Eliot, novelist

It has been proven that pets have a positive effect on our physical and mental health. Having a pet can lower blood pressure and cholesterol levels, reducing the risk of heart disease, and it is very therapeutic for people with mental-health disorders. Pets can help decrease loneliness, and they are great to talk to because they listen without judgment. Stroking and cuddling a pet is healing, and dog-owners tend to be more active than other people because they obtain exercise from walking their pet. The daily care of pets creates a routine that helps to keep our mind-body-spirit healthy.

Music

"Music is a moral law. It gives soul to the universe, wings to the mind, flight to the imagination, a charm to sadness, gaiety and life to everything; It is the essence of order and lends to all that is good, just, and beautiful."

—Plato

Is your mind overactive and constantly whirling with ideas or worries? Soothing music has been shown to raise endorphins and instrumental music that is relaxing has proven to help our outlook, plus provide pain relief and stress relief. I once heard a saying attributed to the Greeks music is an art filled with power to penetrate into the very depths of the soul. When your mind is busy with logic, order, analyzing, and critiquing, you are using the left side of your brain. Try listening to music to use the right side of your brain, which promotes intuition, imagination, color, images, and feelings. Music connects you to a higher state of awareness. Music speaks the language of the heart and it can create an internal transformation. After listening to music you may be astounded by the extraordinary solutions you identify to challenges you have been pondering. Your mind-body-spirit will thank you.

One day as I wrote a letter to my grandmother, it was raining. As I was writing I stopped to listen to the pitter-patter of rain as it fell and I noticed how soothing, calming, and musical it was. I commented in the letter that the rain was making beautiful music. Nature creates music and it is free for everyone to enjoy.

Singing is also a good way to increase your endorphins and it promotes healthy lungs. Put on the tunes and sing along or sing in the shower, which is an excellent way to start your day. Singing and dancing alone or with others is wonderful fun and double the endorphins. (You can even tie together the benefits of pets and music by dancing with your pet, which is also loads of fun. You can disco, jive, hip-hop, or foxtrot and your pet will not rate you like *Dancing with the Stars!*)

Laughter

"God is a comedian playing to an audience too afraid to laugh."
—Voltaire

Is laughter the best medicine? Norman Cousins, author of the book *Anatomy of an Illness as Perceived by the Patient*, certainly thinks it helps. He describes his personal healing and how laughter contributed to his recovery. Research has shown that laughter helps with pain relief, expands happiness, and increases immunity. Research also indicates that laughter is linked to cardiovascular health because it helps to expand tissues to increase blood flow. When we laugh our endorphin levels are higher and laughter is a wonderful coping method for the normal stress of life. "A cheerful heart is good medicine but a crushed spirit dries up the bones." [Proverbs 17:22 (NIV)] There is nothing better than a good belly laugh! Loretta La Roche has an excellent video on *Humor Your Stress* that I have used with groups. A note of caution: if you view the video your cheeks may hurt from laughing. I encourage you to do the actions as you watch.

My friend Yvette is a professional clown and I thought, who better to ask for assistance on the topic of laughter. I asked her what drew her to clowning, and after some contemplation, she responded, "I started clowning because I was wearing a mask, and clowning allowed me to be silly." She was never comfortable being silly, and the clown costume allowed her to be something that she was unable to be. Yvette said she had the strangest occurrences when she was in a crowd of people with her bright wig, big red nose, strange clothes, and big floppy shoes: people would not make eye contact with her; it was as if she did not exist. It is interesting that the attention she craved was denied. She was still invisible and it seemed many in the crowd ignored her display because of their inability to acknowledge silliness. Yvette attended clown school but also learned to have fun and be silly without the mask. Yvette's story is a reminder of the importance to look at what masks we may be wearing. Often the masks are developed as a coping mechanism to protect us from emotional pain. We frequently develop characteristics or roles as a way to be heard or seen. Humor is a wonderful gift when used with the best intentions. If you are using humor to avoid pain or to not be your authentic self, check the messages in your mind and try changing them. Or if you avoid being silly, check those messages too.

When I worked in the Royal Canadian Mounted Police Detachment we ended most days with stories and laughter. Throughout the workday we encountered many tragic events but we were able to find a certain measure of joy despite the circumstances. It was essential that we leave the Detachment each day being positive, or it would have been difficult to return to work the following day knowing that we would encounter similar situations.

Spending time in court listening to horrific events was a component of my work, but even in the courtroom laughter can be found. One day a mental-health expert, Miss Smith, was testifying in court about the mental status of a patient. When it was time for cross-examination, Mr. Jones, a defense lawyer well known for his courtroom antics and who described himself as the courtroom version of MacGyver leapt to within a few feet in front of the witness box. He said, "Well, Miss Smith, I strongly disagree with your assessment because what you just described could also describe my mental state." The judge said, "Mr. Jones, be very careful because from what I have recently witnessed in the courtroom you may personally require the services of Miss Smith." On a daily basis, find something to laugh about, including yourself. Watch a TV or movie comedy, discover a joke, wear something funny to make others laugh, or hang out with some humorous friends.

Intimacy and Sex

"Sex is about sharing and exchanging energies that originate more from our souls than just our heads or our genitals. It is about uniting our longing for wholeness and connection, yearnings that are naturally sacred and spiritual."

—Yoga teacher from New Delhi, India

Kaitlyn, my twelve-year-old niece, asked me, "What does sex have to do with spirituality; it seems like a weird combination." My first thought was *I cannot discuss this with her—she is too young.* Then it dawned on me that it was exactly the right time to discuss the connection because she was interested in hearing my answer and maybe I could teach her the difference between intimacy and sex, especially before she started middle school and learned from her peers. Often when you hear the word *sex* you think of raw passion or slow lovemaking, and the act of sex is rarely considered a spiritual experience. Intimacy usually does not even enter into the dialogue.

In the past, sex was not a topic that was discussed and it was often viewed as something sinful. The topic of sex was often taboo in the church, judgments were made, and the message that got communicated was that sex was wrong. There has been a huge pendulum swing and now everywhere you look sex is used to sell products. The advertisements for ice cream on television imply that eating the product is better than sex and that idea is demonstrated by the person moaning and groaning in ecstasy. Kaitlyn said she gets very tired of everything being turned into a sexual innuendo, and sex is portrayed as something creepy and dirty, but at the same time as an activity that everyone should be doing and that the messages are very confusing.

I hear stories all the time about people hooking up with a partner in the bar and engaging in sexual activities on the first encounter. I am not a prude and I am not making any judgments, but often what you are seeking cannot be found in one-night stands. I have heard countless stories of individuals looking for love and connection and they believe the way to obtain their desire is through sex. When you give yourself away with the intent of being fulfilled by the act of sex, often you feel worse and have added to the baggage in your life. If after the sexual encounter you feel guilt or shame, or you have an expectation of happily ever after, this is not good for your mind-body-spirit. Additionally, if you are engaging in such activities it is vital that you practice safe sex.

You are a whole person and when you engage in any activity you do so with your mind-body-spirit. Sexual contact is filled with energy because it comes from within—it is life's breath inside your body. It is the meeting of flesh and soul and a blending of flesh and spirit. You cannot experience a sexual act without giving something of yourself away, so when you are already lacking or empty it is impossible to be fulfilled by another. You exchange a little bit of your soul with every touch, with every sexual experience.

Intimacy can be obtained by the sharing of one's thoughts and feelings with another person. You can have an intimate relationship with your best friend, your coworker, and your golfing partner without the requirement of sex. Your spirit can be ignited by connecting with the hearts of people all around you. When you connect with others through your heart, the act of sex is a bonus. God provided the glorious gift of sex and it is during this act that conception is achieved. What a wonderful gift to behold the meeting of two souls resulting in the creation of another life force. Is it any wonder that an orgasm produces the most powerful release of endorphins? Just be emotionally, mentally, physically, and spiritually safe without causing harm to yourself or others.

Therapeutic Healing

"Let us be willing to release old hurts."

—Martha Smock, author

When you do not verbally express yourself, your body holds the pain and trauma and when you apply therapeutic touch or healing touch is applied it can unlock the body's memories, thus helping the body to heal physical, mental, and emotional trauma. Therapeutic touch or healing touch has been around for centuries. Healing touch includes but is not limited to such treatments as massage, reiki, reflexology, chiropractic, and Bach flower remedies, etc.

When you give your hand to someone to provide comfort during their time of distress, when they are in either physical or emotional pain, you are providing a healing touch. When you reach out to shake hands in a gesture of welcome, you are providing a healing touch.

The church I attend has a time for Passing of the Peace where we get up from the pews and move about in the church, shaking hands with others and saying, "May the Peace of Christ be with you." It is a welcomed opportunity to connect with the other parishioners, which may not happen if this were not a built-in standard for our service. I suspect that we would rise from our seats at the end of the service and dash out the door to our busy lives, never connecting with anyone, and might end up with the opinion that the church folk are unfriendly because there is no connection. As you become comfortable in the environment the handshakes often turn to hugs and those endorphins love hugs!

Western medicine has started to embrace therapeutic touch and it is now offered in many colleges and universities. healing touch is an act of consciously directing energy through the practitioner in partnership with the person in need of healing. The intention of the practitioner is to give the recipient love and support to overcome physical or psychological problems. Because we do not view ourselves holistically as mind-body-spirit, we create barriers in our body from our denied emotions and mistaken belief systems. When you work in partnership with a practitioner to move the energy blocks within your body, this allows you to explore your mind and the messages you are giving, and you can then change the messages and release the pain that has been holding you back.

When you start to live holistically, and you have an ache or a pain, you will initiate a search of your mind to see if you can make a connection to the pain. We are accustomed to not seeing ourselves as whole, and when our senses encounter something familiar we may feel joy or sorrow and have no idea that the emotion was triggered by a past experience. For example, when you're in the supermarket and someone walks by and your heart starts to race and your knees begin to buckle, it may be because the type of cologne or perfume the person is wearing reminds you of a positive or negative experience in your life. When we are unaware of this potential happening, we can feel like we are going crazy. Often I hear from clients that they dealt with an issue and cannot understand why it is coming up again. You may have mentally explored an issue, but your body is still holding the experience and it needs to be released. Also when you do not use you voice you eat your words, which remain in your body. Healing touch is an opportunity to cleanse your body of waste and free yourself to be whole.

The greatest example in history of the power of healing touch was Jesus. When He physically touched people He broke through isolation and misery. Jesus demonstrated compassion and unity with suffering people. When a leper approached Jesus asking to be healed, Jesus first touched him, an action that meant ritual impurity in Jewish Law (Mark 1:40–45). It was an action of extraordinary compassion. When we follow the teachings of Jesus and provide a loving touch to an individual, we have the ability to transform the spirit.

When you begin to become aware of your mind-body-spirit connection you may trigger memories that you have been ignoring for years. It is important to find either a healing touch practitioner or a counselor who can assist you with your exploration, because it may become overwhelming for you on your own and it is human nature to abandon anything that is painful. When seeking a practitioner it is important that you feel comfortable, and if you do not, then find someone else. Do not judge counseling or healing touch by one experience with a particular service provider, and at the same time be aware of your desire to jump from one service provider to another. Sometimes the tendency is to go shopping for service providers because you do not want your strongly held belief systems and behaviors challenged. Remember you are in charge of your mind-body-spirit health, and do not put practitioners on a pedestal or see them as an expert on you. Only you can determine how far in the healing process you are willing to go. If you embrace the removal of mental and physical barriers, you allow your spirit to shine. There are many forms of alternative health care, and it is important to find the method that is right for you.

Sleep and Rest

"Sleep is the golden chain that ties health and our bodies together."
—Thomas Dekker, English Elizabethan Dramatist

There is nothing better than waking up from a good night's sleep. Sleep keeps your heart healthy and makes you think much more clearly. Lack of sleep can worsen blood pressure and cholesterol and increase your risk of heart attack and stroke. Lack of sleep reduces your endorphin levels. Problem solving is challenging when you lack sleep and your emotions tend be more erratic. Once your endorphin levels are restored you notice that you think more clearly, are slower to anger, feel more at peace and you are more relaxed.

The following are some handy sleep tips:

- Avoid caffeine, nicotine, and alcohol, which suppress deep sleep.

- Avoid heavy meals before bedtime.

- A good mattress can make all the difference in the world to your quality of sleep.

- Establish a bedtime routine. Rushing around completing chores and falling into bed exhausted is not restful.

- If you go straight to bed after watching violence on TV or being in front of the computer, your mind does not have enough time to settle down for a peaceful night's sleep.

- Use your bed for sleeping, not for office work.

- Do not nap before planning to go to bed.

- Write out your "to-do list" before going to bed to help ease your mind.

- Make your bedroom a haven, a welcoming place to unwind.

- Crack your window open a fraction to allow fresh air into your bedroom.

- Keep your bedroom quiet, dark, and cool.

A lack of sleep can be deadly. I have attended numerous fatal car crashes due to the driver's lack of sleep, as verified by police investigation. An individual who tossed and turned in bed all night long may have also been killed due to a lack of sleep, but there is not always adequate information available for confirmation. Please be alert when you drive, or pull over and sleep when necessary. On the flip side, too much sleep can be an avoidance tactic to hide from your thoughts, emotions, and the world; check the messages you are giving yourself and change the CD.

The culture of the modern-day world is to be active for as many of the twenty-four hours as possible. Resting does just not mean sleeping. Taking a quiet minute or three throughout the day will rejuvenate your mind-body-spirit. Try eliminating all communication devices and electronic games, etc., for one day; you will be surprised at how peaceful your surroundings will be. If you are constantly filling your life with activities and noise, when do you have time to hear the messages that God is trying to share? After we have encountered a new learning we value hindsight, and it is obtained by stepping back from the situation and reflecting. If you give yourself pauses and breaks, you will have insight into situations and save yourself some steps along the way.

Many individuals have difficulty with rest because they believe that rest equals laziness. Jill, a participant in one of my programs, really struggled with the idea of rest.

Jill was always active. When Jill stopped she would either fall asleep or her mind would be whirling with all the things she could be accomplishing. During Jill's childhood she received the message that if she was not active she was being lazy. Once Jill changed her beliefs surrounding rest, she eliminated some activities and electronics from her life. Jill was able to center her being and she gained new insights and discovered peace. She now seeks rest and her mind-body-spirit thrives. Her new calculation is Rest = Rejuvenation, Revitalization, and Regeneration.

Even God rested on the seventh day!

Deep Breathing

For breath is life, and if you breathe well
you will live long on earth.

—Sanskrit Proverb

During times of stress you unconsciously hold your breath, but oxygenating is essential to the health of your mind-body-spirit. Deep breathing helps to release endorphins. The upward and downward movement of the diaphragm helps to remove toxins from our system and promotes better blood flow. When we deeply draw oxygen in we nourish our body, so out with the old and draw in the fresh and new.

Often when my mother contacts me by telephone, immediately after I say hello she launches into a monologue about whatever is on her mind, she runs one sentence into the next, and sometimes changes topics without taking a breath. I can feel myself holding my breath as she speaks, and sometimes I have updated information pertinent to what she's saying or I have heard the story already from another source. When she finally finishes, I give myself a breath and then I share my new information with her, and she wonders why I never said anything before. In my mother's era a child was "seen and not heard" and that translated to her that she could not have a voice. The CD never changed as she grew, resulting in my mother believing that she did not have a right to share her opinion with others. Over time, she intellectually realized that she could have a voice and an opinion, but she did not connect mind-body-spirit; therefore when she had the opportunity to speak, she broke like a water main with no shutoff valve.

I heard Michael J. Tamura, spiritual teacher, healer, and clairvoyant, speak at a conference, and he stated that we tell ourselves to "take a breath," but he encourages us to "give ourselves a breath" instead. Inhale a deep cleansing breath and exhale fully. Now try inhaling from the bottom of your stomach and exhale fully. My mother did not believe that she was worthy to give herself a breath, and unconsciously she believed it to be a selfish act. Tamura's words are important because giving ourselves a breath is a much more loving act than taking a breath. As you inhale, you receive a loving life gift from God versus taking something from Him; whichever way you view it, the most important thing is to do it.

When I was in grade one, I would write my sentences with no punctuation, and I read the same way. My teacher explained that a period was an opportunity to take a breath. I had not considered it an option because I wrote and spoke the way my mind worked, which was continuous. This was a very new concept for me, and as I read aloud and paused at the end of each sentence to give myself a breath, I guess I was taking too long of a breath because the teacher thought I did not know the following word, and would help me out. This is a prime example of what happens when we begin to make changes in our lives, we will swing like a pendulum because it is new, and we must find our way back to the center to obtain balance. Giving ourselves a breath allows us to collect our thoughts and feelings, and to recognize the messages our mind-body-spirit is sending, which makes us centered and balanced; it is an essential ingredient to reliable decision-making.

After teaching a lesson on this theme, the following week as we were doing the group check-in and one of the female participants stated she got a lot out of the breathwork lesson. She was taking deep cleansing breaths during stressful situations. She said it was really helping her to not use her voice when she had something to share. That, of course, was not the lesson I intended to teach! I immediately thought, Well I need to rework the lesson plan. I asked her what her thoughts were when we were doing the lesson. She said, "I was remembering the past when I was told I interrupted all the time." I had her take a few deep cleansing breaths and I repeated some of the material. I asked her what she got from the information and she heard something new, and thankfully it was closer to the point I had been trying to make. It is important to continue to check the messages you are receiving because when you are replaying the old CD you miss new music.

"It was my secretary's fault. She forgot
to put breathing on my to-do list."

Chapter Review:

- Start by choosing one activity that you will incorporate into your life on a regular basis to increase your endorphin levels.

- Make a mental note or journal any changes you notice in your life. Are you feeling more joyous, less stressed, etc.?

- Do not stop doing the activities in Chapter 1; build on each of the techniques like stepping stones.

- Add to your toolbox a bottle of water, soft music, a joke, something from nature, nutritional snacks, etc.

⁓ 3 ⁓

Meditation

If you would leave your daily tasks
And set an hour aside,
To empty out a worried mind
And let sweet silence come inside.
There are blessings in this silence
To refresh you and renew
The strength and calmness of the spirit
A loving God has given to you.
Such an hour is never wasted
Nor its wonder fade away
As you rise, with peace and calmness,
To the demands of each new day.

—Lillian Bennett Armstrong

*"Plant the seed of meditation and reap the
fruit of peace of mind."*

—Remez Sasson, author, creator, and owner of
www.SuccessConsciousness.com

SCIENTISTS HAVE RECENTLY FOUND that in addition to calming the nerves and reducing blood pressure, the regular practice of meditation helps the body produce endorphins for a feeling of well-being.

Over the years, I have found meditation to be one of the most difficult techniques for individuals to grasp and to incorporate on a regular practice. I too find it difficult. I read material on the Internet about meditation and I tried it myself, but still struggled to quiet the mind. Sometimes I was able to find peace, but it was a constant challenge and I was uncertain if it was me or if maybe meditation did not work as well as advertised. It was not until I attended film night at the local auditorium that meditation was really brought to my attention. The film was *Unmistaken Child*, a documentary about a Buddhist monk and his search for the reincarnation of his master. As I approached the table to pay, a Buddhist nun handed me a flyer and said, "Here, you need this," and her voice appeared to be coming through a megaphone. As I sat in my seat I turned the flyer over and it was announcing an introduction class on meditation. I thoroughly enjoyed the film because it challenged my thinking, but what really intrigued me was the meditation class and I immediately decided that I needed to attend.

The class was held one evening per week for five weeks for two hours, and that same Buddhist nun facilitated the class. When I attended the class I realized that I was not alone in my struggle, as often is the case. Many people had been struggling to learn on their own via books and CDs, but could not find peace. A few individuals had attended previous meditation classes and they had been practicing meditation for many months but took the class again to help them get back on track because they did not have a consistent practice.

When you begin meditation, choose a quiet space in your home or outside for your regular meditation practice. Select a regular time for practice that best suits your needs and schedule. You need to be able to sit comfortably on the floor or in a chair. If you are sitting on the floor, ensure that you have a cushion under your buttocks, and if you are sitting cross-legged, place pillows so you can rest your knees on them for more physical comfort. If you are sitting in a chair, place your feet on the floor and ensure that your back is erect—no slouching.

Place your hands in your lap, with palms facing upward, one hand cupping the other, with your thumbs touching and pointed toward your belly button. Close your eyes, and bow your head slightly, with your chin tilted toward your chest. Give yourself three deep cleansing breathes, exhaling fully. Now scan your body and locate the tension spots and breathe air into those spots, releasing the tension. Place your tongue at the roof of your mouth behind your teeth and breathe naturally. Focus on breathing in through your nose and out through your mouth.

You may have thoughts entering your mind, such as grocery shopping, rush-hour traffic, whether your spouse remembered to pick up the dry cleaning—any annoyances or worries that occurred throughout the day. You may hear noises outside, like a dog barking, a rooster crowing, or children laughing. You may notice aches and pains in your body. When this happens, notice the thoughts, sounds, and pain, but do not attach to them; let them go like watching the clouds pass by, and go directly back to observing your breath. Every time a thought, sound, or pain enters, notice it, but do not attach, and go back to breath work. Initially you may fall asleep because your body is so exhausted and this is the first opportunity you've had to rest, and if you do fall asleep it is okay. If falling asleep seems to be a common practice, ensure that your posture is erect and your head is only slightly bent. You will naturally feel when you are finished with the meditation session, and will you gently open your eyes, slowly shaking your hands and feet.

As I practiced the technique at home, it became easier. My mind was quieting and I was finding peace. As the weeks progressed the nun introduced us to several methods of meditation, and it is important to have a toolkit available when you need it and because everyone connects with something different. She familiarized us with techniques requiring us to visualize the ocean, and she assisted with conflict resolution. The nun had us visualize someone we hated and what it would take for us to find compassion for them. I visualized Cheryl, a work colleague whom I strongly disliked, as I do not allow hate to fill my being. I found Cheryl to be annoying because she presented herself as a know-it-all, and I considered her loud and obnoxious. Then I visualized Cheryl experiencing the death of a loved one and I found great compassion for her. The nun had us visualize someone we loved and what it would take to end the relationship. I visualized

Heather, my best friend, having an affair with my husband and I was able to feel tremendous betrayal and anger. The realization from the meditation was that our mind is very powerful and even though neither of those situations actually occurred, I was able to feel the emotions very strongly because my mind could not tell the difference between the truth and my imagination. I also realized that it was not difficult to find compassion for someone whom I disliked. My heart was open to my colleague and how I interacted with her changed from that day forward. As for my best friend, we had a great laugh about her part in the exercise.

The three most important things that I learned about meditation were practice, practice, practice. It is vital that you set time aside every day for meditation, even if it is only five to ten minutes per day. You will most likely need five minutes to get your mind to settle; any shorter, and you may have a hard time recognizing the benefit. Daily practice allows the technique to transform into peacefulness and it can become as habitual as brushing your teeth.

The class was presented to me at exactly the right time because I was burning out from life, but especially work, and I was struggling with a very active mind. Growing up I developed the ability to plan, and I never had just one back-up plan—I usually had at least five ready to roll out at a moment's notice. It was a survival skill that I learned as a young child growing up in an alcoholic home. I turned the survival skill into a very wonderful career, but as I progressed in life that same skill was taking a toll on my overall health. As a practitioner working with clients in crisis, having the ability to rapidly jump from one plan to another was an asset to my career. What was starting to wear me down was my very active mind. I lost the ability to shut it off when I left work; my mind was constantly whirling with ideas and worries about the past, present and the future while rehashing scenarios I had encountered throughout the day. The daily practice of meditation allowed me to finally settle my mind, which had been overactive for as long as I could remember. I was unable to recall a time in my life that my mind was not busy with some worry or plan. The quietness was a completely new concept for me, but a refreshing one.

No two incidents of meditation will be the same; each time is a new journey. Sometimes you will meditate for a few minutes and other times it may be closer to an hour. If and when you have a *wow* moment, it is essential that you not look for it the next time you meditate; you may not find it, but the tendency is to go looking. Please do not force yourself to have these same experiences, because you will begin to become frustrated and will most likely abandon the practice of meditation. There will be times that you can quickly settle the mind, and you may be able to repeat this over and over, yet on another day it is a challenge once again. Do not be concerned; this is normal and the key is to return to the breath work—always go back to the breath work.

As you become more familiar with meditation try adding some exercises into your practice. I found a practical exercise from the book *A Path with Heart: A Guide Through the Perils and Promises of Spiritual Life*, by Jack Kornfield, to be very helpful. When meditating visualize a problem or issue that you are having. Now invite Jesus or Buddha or whatever you believe into your problem and your body and ask that spiritual leader to deal with the issue. You need to step out of your body to watch that spiritual leader deal with the problem in the manner that they choose. Your only role is to watch.

When I did this meditation I had recently quit my job and sold my house, and there were no concrete plans for the future. I started worrying about my financial obligations and the future because having no plans was completely uncharacteristic of me. I invited Jesus into my problem and my body. I observed him in my body and recognized my clothes, but knew that it was Him because He stood with His arms at His side, palms extended forward. Jesus's head began to rapidly turn from side to side like an agitator in a washing machine. As I watched the scene for what seemed to be a very long time, I heard the word *patience* and I relaxed as I continued to observe Him. After some time passed, His head began to slow and eventually stopped turning and I heard the words *Be Silent, Be Still.* I opened my eyes knowing that those were exactly the actions I needed to take. My head had felt like a washing-machine agitator and I knew that the answers were there, but I was not incorporating my knowledge. Now when my mind begins a new cycle, I stop, give myself a breath, remember to be silent and still and to have patience, and I immediately stop the cycle and feel very peaceful.

Use meditation to calm your mind, relax your body, and connect with your spirit. Listen to your mind-body-spirit to help you heal your life!

Chapter Review:

- Create a comfortable space for meditation.

- Schedule time for meditation daily.

- Practice, practice, practice.

- Try incorporating different exercises into your meditation once you are familiar with basic meditation practices.

☙ 4 ❧

Forgiveness

"Forgiveness is choosing to love. It is the first skill of self-giving love."

—Mahatma Gandhi

"Let us forgive each other – only then will we live in peace."

—Leo Tolstoy, Russian writer

FORGIVENESS IS A NASTY WORD, but someone needs to say it and do it. Whenever I facilitated self-esteem workshops we would review various ways to increase self-esteem. As we read through the list of examples, like being appreciative, doing something nice for yourself and others , etc., everyone would be in agreement. As we moved down the list I waited with a secret smile for forgiveness to appear on the paper and each time I was not disappointed. Every time, without fail, I heard one or more individuals chime, "No I cannot forgive," which started a lively conversation about forgiveness. Forgiveness is not the same as forgetting; forgiveness is a gift to yourself.

Dr. Fred Luskin, director and cofounder of the Stanford University Forgiveness Project and author of *Forgive for Good: A Proven Prescription for Health and Happiness*, has successfully researched and documented how forgiveness improves our emotional and physical well-being. He says, "When we rent too much space to disappointment we create a grievance story." What is your grievance story?

Ralph was bitter and angry because life was not fair; he had many grievance stories. His ex-wife cheated on him, his bosses disliked him, the bank was not being reasonable about finance charges, his children never visited, he had no friends, and his childhood was rotten. Ralph went to the bar several times a week to tell his grievance story, and he often found willing listeners until they realized the story never changed; slowly they too would abandon him. Each time Ralph told his story, it was with the same energy, as if it had just occurred. Ralph refused to see that he was creating his current circumstances. The past was long gone, but in Ralph's mind it was thriving. He would not take responsibility for his reaction to the events that occurred in his life, which resulted in others refusing to interact with him. How much energy are you losing to your grievance story?

One night as I slept, an idea about forgiveness was provided to me, and when I woke I could remember the first and last parts; I wrote them down. As I went for my morning walk, I stopped partway down the driveway because the middle part was coming back to me. When I turned I saw my husband going into the travel trailer, and he returned with a pen and paper. I finished the phrasing: "I wear grudges like a badge of honor. Forgiveness does not enter into the equation, and I refuse to give it over to God in prayer." This idea turned out to be important. A woman named Anita visited my office after being pushed by her spouse, and he was arrested for intimate-partner violence. Anita shared her surprise regarding her spouse's arrest, and I explained the British Columbia Violence against Women in Relationships policy to her, and the mandatory arrest of individuals suspected of violence. I also reviewed material on abuse with her, and when I explained she was the victim on the police file, her eyes got big and she said, "That's right. I am a victim." I could tell that she was very attached to the word *victim*; I explained that she did not need to remain a victim. But Anita loved the word *victim*, and it became her new identity. When she attended court, Anita announced with pride to anyone who would listen that she was a victim. The offender pled guilty, but the real legal fight was just beginning in civil court over the division of property and child maintenance. Anita wore victimization like a badge of honor, and would argue over everything. She could not hear when her ex-spouse offered reasonable solutions to property division because she was attached to her disappointments. Over ten years later, the court battle continues. Anita now represents herself in court because she fired every lawyer who tried to help her. She is attached to her grievance story. Anita is an example of how a grievance story can take over your life and rob you of the joy of living in the present. What is robbing you from living your best life?

Many domestic-violence victims came into my office shortly after their spouse had been arrested, seeking to change the no-contact conditions on the police release order. Our policy was to provide education on the topic before assisting with the paperwork. Almost one hundred percent of the time when I asked why they wanted the release conditions changed, I heard "I love him/her and I forgive my partner." When I explored forgiveness with the client, I found that it was about forgetting, not forgiving, and they wanted their partner home to fulfill financial or parenting obligations or because they were afraid to be alone.

It is important that you grieve your loss, whether it is the death of a loved one or unfulfilled expectations. You need to go through the stages of grief which have been described as denial, anger, bargaining, depression, and acceptance. There is no script for grief and we can feel our emotions in any particular order. It is okay to be angry at the other person, the deceased, or God, because it is part of the grief process. Being angry at God is acceptable; it is not wicked. When Jesus was on the cross, He cried out in a loud voice to God, "My God, my God, why have you forsaken me?" [Mark 15:34 (NIV)]. The crucial goal is to not get trapped in your heartache. When our children get angry with us, we continue to love them and want the best for them. We are God's children, and He loves us unconditionally. What or who do you need to grieve? Are you caught in any of the grief stages? What do you need to accept?

A quote I received by email (unfortunately I have no idea whose inspiration it was) was quite enlightening:

"What hurts so much in you that you feel the need to hurt others?" When you can see the other person's pain, it can change your perspective. I worked with a Restorative Justice group who focused on cases such as mischief, common assault, and theft. Restorative justice utilizes the process of "healing circles" as used by the Maori in New Zealand. Restorative justice is the repair of relationships and a formal meeting is facilitated between the offender, the victim, and their respective families and/or supporters. It allows offenders to accept responsibility for their behavior and the group determines how best to repair the harm. The impact on the offenders was amazing because when performing the crimes they gave no consideration to the outcome of their actions. Many times a victim developed compassion for an offender because the meeting provided an opportunity for storytelling and both parties learned to see where the other person was coming from. This type of exchange created healing for all involved. What comes to mind is that old saying, "Walk a mile in the other person's shoes." Are you able to put yourself in the other's shoes or see the others person's pain?

As my mother and I were having lunch one day, she told me I had a lot of wisdom. She realized when I was growing up I was often the adult, not her. For years I had longed for this acknowledgement, but after she finished speaking, I casually brushed the matter aside. I could see disappointment on her face, and I felt a bit ashamed of my behavior. When I took time to reflect on the situation, I realized I was protecting myself from being hurt. Sometimes my mother would have profound insight, and I would get very excited because I thought she was "getting it," but soon I was hit with another disappointing comment. I often felt that I wanted more for my mother than she wanted for herself. I forgave my father and many others for what I considered much worse transgressions, but I would not forgive my mother; she was my grievance story.

I started working on opening my heart to her, but it was during another instance of sharing many months later that I had one of those moments of clarity that could come only from God. My mother was explaining to one of her grandchildren that she did not have a voice growing up, and it continued into her adult life. She taught all of her children not to have a voice, and now her oldest daughter was teaching her, she said, which is not the order of parenting, but often the child becomes the teacher. It was at that moment I realized the logical order of parenting would be for the child to learn from the parent, but spiritual parenting was different, and the child being the teacher was also natural. Any remaining animosity left me at that moment. Please do not beat up yourself or anyone else about the past. People do the best they can with the information and tools available to them at the time.

In 2008 I attended a conference in Edmonton, Alberta for families of homicide victims, and it was a very heart-touching event. I attended one workshop with a panel of speakers that included a warden from a correctional institute, an offender who was on parole for murder, and a mother whose son was killed by an offender who was still incarcerated. The purpose of the panel was to share a Corrections program called Victim-Offender Reconciliation.

An offender would meet families and groups to hear the pain caused to families of homicide victims. Then the offender would share his story. This exchange created an opportunity for both parties to heal and grow. During the panel the parolee shared his story of how he murdered a stranger during a drunken rampage. He informed the audience, "There is not a day that goes by I do not think about my actions and the pain I caused." As he took questions from the audience, one person stood and thanked him for his openness and said that for the first time in five years she could feel herself starting to heal. She was unable to meet the person who killed her brother. The woman stated that she just realized that when her brother was murdered not only was her family shattered, but so was the family of the offender. The woman went on to state that she no longer had the desire to meet her brother's killer because she realized she needed to release the shackles that bound her.

Probably one of the most difficult things to forgive is the homicide of your child, and that's what makes the story of a man named James so profound. James's son Randy was killed by his best friend during a stupid drunken brawl. Within a week of the homicide James was sharing his thoughts about the need to forgive the offender, which is highly unusual in my line of work. The father of the deceased does not normally bring up the topic, especially so soon after his son's death. James needed to forgive the offender not for the offender's sake, but for his own. He said, that if he held on to the anger, it would destroy him. James was in recovery for alcohol addiction and has been successfully working his twelve-step AA program for years. James said, he lost his son, but he did not want to lose his recovery to the offender too. James spoke of the need for forgiveness at his AA meetings and anywhere else he could find an audience. He especially wanted to reach the youth and young adults in the community. He was often confronted by people who could not understand how he could be speaking about forgiveness, because the death of a child is an unforgiveable sin. He stood strong and tall during these moments and with great patience shared that the forgiveness was for *his* healing not the offender's.

James attended every court appearance, and he met with the prosecutors to discuss the case and informed them that he wanted the offender to have substantial jail time for the offense; he was able to forgive but still request justice for an unjust act. James did not instantly find forgiveness. He worked at it. When meeting with James, I could see his struggle, but as time went on I started to notice a peaceful expression come over his entire being. He found forgiveness by working his twelve-step program, and in return he found inner peace.

What made James stand out from many clients I worked with was his immediate need to begin the dialogue of forgiveness, and his complete understanding that the requirement was for his own health. He was able to separate society's views from his own to maintain his path to forgiveness. James did not expect the legal system to make him feel better; he took charge of his health, and his spirit shines brightly. James's story is an outstanding example of forgiveness, but the original act was completed by God—He too forgave for the murder of a son.

There are many techniques you can utilize for forgiveness. You do not need to meet with the person who harmed you to forgive. Sometimes it is helpful to write a letter to the other person, and then burn it. You can simply tell God who and what needs forgiveness, including yourself. Like in James's situation, support groups may be helpful. Meditation is also a useful tool. You may not be able to obtain feelings of forgiveness immediately, but keep working at it and it will happen. The pain you feel is real, but remember it is not hurting the other person—it is hurting you. The book *Prayers of the Cosmos—Reflections on the Original Meaning of Jesus's Words*, by Neil Douglas-Klotz, recovers the original Middle Eastern language, the Aramaic language that Jesus spoke. Each Aramic word presents several possible translations such as "Blessed are the meek, for they shall inherit the earth" and one possible Aramaic translation could be "Blessed are those who have softened the rigidity within."

One night I could not sleep and decided that I needed to get out of bed and meditate. I began my usual meditation practice, and as I scanned my body for tension, I explored what was blocked in my body. As I noticed the stiffness in my knees, I heard the most loving and gentle voice tell me that I needed to "Forgive." I started taking an inventory of all the people and issues that needed forgiveness in my life. I started with easy stuff like the time I took money from my mother's wallet without her permission, hitting my brother on the head with a plastic baseball bat but telling everyone it was an accident, and cheating on an elementary-school test. As I forgave myself for each transgression, God said, "Next." I moved on to forgiving my coworkers for the pain I thought they had inflicted on me and for the pain I had inflicted on them. As I moved up my body, I could feel fear rising, and God said, "I am with you," and "You are loved," and "You can do it." I felt engulfed by love. When there were some things that I did not want to face, He said, "You can do it." I felt physically ill, but I continued because I knew that this was a very special moment. I finally looked at sexual abuse. I had forgiven the abuser a long time ago, but I was still holding myself responsible. I knew intellectually that a child is not responsible for sexual abuse, but my body was not on the same page. I wanted to turn back, but God said, "I am here." When I was finally able to forgive myself, my chest began to hurt, and for a moment I thought I was having a heart attack, but I knew that God did not walk me through this process for it to end in a heart attack. It felt like my chest was cracking and breaking, but soon the pain subsided and I could feel warmth, love, and tremendous compassion, and my heart felt like it was the size of the ocean. I felt joy and peace. Eventually I opened my eyes, but the most exciting occurrence was the opening of my heart.

I have not been the same since that meditation exercise; I had a truly blessed moment. My heart was opened that night, and I began to love the world in a whole new way. I felt differently about myself and others. I had incredible joy, but also tremendous sadness when I saw people in pain. I believed that I was a compassionate person before this experience, but I reached an entirely new level of concern for others and I truly loved myself in a generous way. I had difficulty remembering all the people and issues I forgave, not because they were minor, but because I no longer had any attachment to the cause and I had no pain. The issue was completely removed from my system. I understood why I needed to forgive myself for the sexual abuse because as a child I blamed myself, and although my mind understood, I still held the belief deep within my body and it was affecting my spirit.

I encourage you to try this meditation; you may not have Divine guidance, but I was given this exercise to open my heart and to share with others God's teaching. Simply meditate in the usual manner, notice the blockages in your body, and take inventory of the people and events that need forgiveness, including yourself. Inhale deep cleansing breaths; fully exhale when you feel tension or fear. Remember that God is always with you, even if you cannot hear His voice during the exercise. Know that His words are the same for you as they were for me. Repeat the meditation as many times as needed to complete your inventory and to fully forgive. Periodically, perform this exercise, because it is like cleaning your closet. Things build up and need to be removed, or something was hidden in the back we did not notice, and some things are misplaced or mislabeled—time changes things and sometimes items do not fit like they once did or that sentimental item that you do not want to release is less painful and you may be ready to look at it and give it away. Do not allow yourself to become rigid. Allow God to walk with you; let Him carry your pain.

When Ginger was asked if she had a grievance story she said, "Yes, my now-deceased husband cheated on me during our marriage and I still struggle with being jealous of the other woman." She knew it was robbing her of living her best life. When asked where she held the issue in her body, she said it was in her stomach and she held up a fist; it was turning white from her grip. She said, "I am stuck in grief at the Anger stage." When asked if she could see what was hurting in the other woman, Ginger said, "I realized the woman was lacking and maybe something happened in her past. She craved attention and this was the only way for her to get it." When Ginger recalled the scenario, it was thriving. She said, "I wish I had spoken up at the time and at least voiced my feelings and opinions." I asked her who or what she needed to forgive. Ginger instantly said she needed to forgive herself. Her eyes got huge; she stated that the realization was a big surprise. She said, "I thought the affair was my fault. I believed if only I had been a better person, or thinner, or more attractive, or had more time to spend with my husband it would not have happened."

As she performed the meditation exercise her entire body was tense and her jaw was clenched. Then suddenly her body went limp and she opened her eyes. Ginger reported that she felt the tension, then energy rushed up her leg and her body released as she found forgiveness. She felt lighter, and when asked about the incident she did not feel any anger and the matter was gone. Her complexion improved and she appeared peaceful. Ginger was encouraged to give herself several deep cleansing breaths and to drink plenty of water after the exercise because it would help to flush toxins out of her body. Ginger had not yet completed an entire inventory, but her mind would begin to seek other scenes, and she needed to be properly oxygenated and hydrated to deal with any tension that may arise from further thoughts.

Since your body consists of seventy percent water and you have been packing debris for a while, the water in your body is muddy and you need to fill your body with new clear water.

Please do not be concerned about being "too bad," "too rotten," "too wicked," or "too damaged" to be forgiven, because God has not disowned you and He has already forgiven you. Forgiveness is not something God requires of you; the need to forgive and to be forgiven is for your own healing. God walked me through the forgiveness activity because He understood my needs. Remember you are engulfed with love as you forgive others and yourself.

Chapter Review:

- What is your grievance story?

- Who or what do you need to forgive?

- Take an inventory.

- Find a way to begin the forgiveness process.

5

Love

"A Candle is Burning"
by Sandra Dean

A candle is burning, a flame warm and bright, a candle of hope in December's dark night. While angels sing blessings from heaven's starry sky, our hearts we prepare now for Jesus is nigh.

A candle is burning, a candle of peace, a candle to signal that conflict must cease: for Jesus is coming to show us the way; a message of peace humbly laid in the hay.

A candle is burning, a candle of joy, a candle to welcome brave Mary's new boy. Our hearts fill with wonder and eyes light and glow as joy brightens winter like sunshine on snow. A candle is burning, a candle of love, a candle to point us to heaven above. A baby for Christmas, a wonderful birth, for Jesus is bringing God's love to our earth.

We honour our Messiah with Christ candle's flame, our Christmas Eve candles glad tidings proclaim. O come, all you faithful, rejoice in this night, as God comes among us, the Christian's true light.

"If I have the gift of prophecy and can fathom all mysteries and all knowledge, and if I have a faith that can move mountains, but have not love, I am nothing. If I give all my possessions to the poor and surrender my body to the flames, but have not love, I gain nothing."

—1 Corinthians 13:2–3 (NIV)

WHAT IS LOVE? Love is being heart-conscious. I first learned of the phrase *heart-consciousness* in the book *Prayers of the Cosmos—Reflections on the Original Meaning of Jesus's Words*, by Neil Douglas-Klotz, and I immediately realized that it was exactly what was missing from my vocabulary to describe the purpose of life. I tried describing loving yourself, loving God, and loving the world, but no term better describes the meaning than *heart-consciousness*. Heart-consciousness is the supreme way of life, the way that never fails, the way that leads to God's prearranged purpose; it is love.

The formula or the road map for heart-consciousness was provided in the New Testament of the Bible in 1 Corinthians 13:4–7 (NIV):

"Love is patient, love is kind. It does not envy, it does not boast, it is not proud. It is not rude, it is not self-seeking, it is not easily angered, it keeps no record of wrongs. Love does not delight in evil but rejoices with the truth. It always protects, always trusts, always hopes, and always perseveres."

Love is impossible to explain because it is so expansive and complete, but the way to love can be explained through the following philosophies:

Patience: Patience is generous. When you encounter a difficult person who is being rude or uppity, you can retaliate or become rude or develop a grievance story or you can be generous of spirit and offer self-restraint.

Kindness: Kindness is action. Sharing a smile, a kind word, a helping hand, is free, and it has a ripple effect throughout the world. When you smile you can change the mood of the person you meet, and that in turn can change how they behave toward another, like ripples in a pond or the "pay it forward" movement.

Envy and boasting: Envy is self-focused or inward-focused. In a world that is focused on material possessions it is difficult not to desire what others have, but when you can rejoice in and appreciate the good qualities and successes of others you will be abundant in spirit. Boasting and pride are outward expressions of inward uncertainty. When someone flaunts her successes or materialism or toots her own horn, she needs compassion because something is lacking within. When your spirit is filled, you are modest and humble.

Rudeness and self-seeking: When someone is talking and you want to jump in with your thoughts and opinions, you are not listening because you have this desire to be heard yourself; therefore you are concentrating on your own opportunity to speak. It is a rude behavior just like when you interrupt someone when speaking. When you are focused on yourself you lose that precious gift of giving and receiving.

Anger: Anger is the outward expression of hurt. When we allow petty aggravations and frustrations to affect us we become irritable and we do not have peace of mind. Anger has been the cause of much unhappiness; it has wrecked friendships, ruined marriages, destroyed families, broken or shattered relationships, and affected the workplace. Other characteristics are sarcasm, sullenness, or brooding and resentment. When you are cantankerous it leads to displays of anger. There is righteous anger against sin and all injustice, but actions can be loving and peaceful.

No records of wrong: We do not embrace memories or grievance stories of crimes personally suffered (no keeping score). When we engage in gossip or scandal we are assisting others with the creation of a toxic environment it is a platform for grievance stories. By not stopping the exchange we are rejoicing in the failures and follies of others. When you contribute to gossip it makes it difficult for individuals to get along and record keeping begins. When you have the urge to engage in gossip, ask yourself: Is it true? Is it necessary to share the story? Is it kind? It will help you and others to eliminate the score card.

Rejoicing in truth: Always be eager to hear and believe the best in others. Encourage others to do well—children, especially, shine with support. Every one of us is a child of God and we benefit when we give and receive support.

Protect: When Rev. Dr. Martin Luther King, Jr. led the Freedom March he took on the problems of his race and country; he did not *need* to get involved, and he was not *required* to lead the process; he took on the burdens and injustices of others. This is the highest expression of love. There are still many injustices in our current time, like victims of crime lacking a voice, world hunger, environmental issues, etc., and there are many opportunities for you to speak against the harm being done to others, whether it is in your home, your community, your nation, or on a global level.

Trust: Believe in possibility. When someone is a helper of the church or the community that person can become weary from the work because there is so much pain, injustice, and lack of peace. Plus, people often decline the help. It could be easy to become bitter and disillusioned, but when you trust the love of God you find a way to keep the flame burning. You may change the way you provide service, but you continue to deliver the message.

Hope: Hope for the best even when it is logically difficult to find it. Sometimes things must be broken to reveal the beauty. An egg cracks for a baby chick to emerge, the ground opens for a sprout to appear, family units are fractured for new ones to be formed, burnout happens for the purpose of life to be found. Often people must hit rock bottom for positive change to occur, and each person has a different rock bottom. Each one of us has pieces broken inside us; God is waiting for an awakening to take place.

Preserve: Love never disappears. Divine love is eternal. Even though Jesus knew that Judas Iscariot was going to betray Him, Judas was offered bread soaked in wine because love does not end. When someone dies, we continue to love them even though they are not with us— the very popular saying, "They are always in your heart" is true. We are always loved by God. There is nothing that we can do for Him to abandon us. After all, God's son was killed and His love for everyone remained.

The scriptures of 1 Corinthians 13:4–7 (NIV) are probably the most used words from the Bible for the exchange of wedding vows, but it is not a road map for newlyweds, but rather a blueprint for all human beings. It seems that not long into a marriage these words are forgotten or we lose sight of our path, just as we did growing up. It is not too late to remember and to use this as our compass in life's journey!

A woman named Jasmine realized she did not understand love. She entered into every relationship, whether it was with friends, romantic partners, or coworkers, seeking to serve them. Jasmine thought love was about giving herself up to others. She believed the more she fulfilled their needs, the more love she would receive in return. Jasmine could not understand why she was always being hurt by others when she was so generous and loving. She was outwardly generous, but she had an inward feeling of lack. Jasmine measured her self-worth by the thoughts, actions, and words of others. Jasmine was unconsciously asking, what's in it for me? She was doing the "generous acts" to fill a need within her being. When Jasmine started to love herself the feeling of lack diminished, she no longer felt hurt and she stopped basing her self-worth on others.

Love is not something you achieve by doing good deeds; it is something you discover when you go within. When you model love and then you do acts of love, your feelings and actions must be congruent. When you have stormy relationships, check your messages and actions for consistency because when you value yourself, others value you too. Remember: you are lovable because God created you that way!

Chapter Review:

- Explore your level of heart-consciousness.
- Choose one or two philosophies to work on.
- Notice the results.

6

Blessings

**"Lord, we thank thee for the
bounty we're about to receive."**

*"Our prayers should be blessings in general, for God knows
best what is good for us."*

—Socrates

COUNTING YOUR BLESSINGS SOUNDS simple
enough. Saying "thank you" is a component of eti-
quette, but are you on autopilot? Do you take a moment
to really appreciate the blessings that are presented to you

each and every day? When you are heart-conscious you see the beauty and abundance all around you. When you are suffering it is difficult to see the abundance. For instance, if you are financially strapped, often everything around you appears to be lacking. We tend to spend too much time in our mind, trying to figure our way out of the financial discord and everywhere we look we see events and items that cost money, which remind us of our misfortune. It is challenging to create positive thinking when it is a struggle to survive. You could fake it until you make it, and that may work or you can get spiritually connected so it does work. When you open your heart your eyes see what your heart sees. The money burdens lessen because all feels right with your spirit.

Sometimes the people who notice blessings the most are the homeless because a kind word or gesture or smile means more to them than to others. They are not caught up in the craziness to climb the corporate ladder or to outdo the neighbor, because they are learning to survive on what is offered to them. When I volunteered for the Salvation Army Christmas Kettle Campaign, I often knew many of the contributors because I live in a small community. It always touched my heart when people shared that they once survived by using the food bank, and they recognized the importance of giving. Because I worked in the social-service sector, I knew the background of many of the contributors and I was always in awe of how many people with no disposable income would deposit their last bit of change or whatever they could into the kettle.

Often when people become seriously ill you hear about life-changing transformations because they have learned to appreciate all the blessings that surround them. I attended a conference where Dr. Jill Bolte Taylor, PhD, author of *My Stroke of Insight,* was the keynote speaker. She described her stroke and recovery. Each morning in silent prayer and gratitude she says to her cells, "Thank you for waking me up today." I too gained a new appreciation for the gift of life, and every morning I shout with joy, "I am alive" and it is a wonderful start to the day. When I have low energy, I repeat the phrase, and I continue to repeat it until my voice actually sounds blessed, saying the quote in a lackluster tone is just too dreary and it seems insincere.

Take yourself off autopilot and start noticing the many blessings that God provided absolutely free. Notice the sun shining, the birds signing; a baby's smile; children laughing; flowers blooming; the soothing and musical sound of the rain; the smell of fresh-cut grass; the calm fluffiness of new-fallen snow; the changing color of the leaves; fresh water; clean air; the natural talents you have been given; the ability to walk, speak, smell, see, taste, feel, touch, and to use your imagination.

I live in Canada and a favorite pastime here is to discuss or complain about the weather. It is too cold, too hot, there's not enough rain, too much rain, etc. During one particular rainy month my young niece, Megan, informed me that she was tired of people complaining about the rain because, "Could they not remember the previous year when there were so many forest fires that you could not go outside, due to the poor air quality?" She said she loves the smell of the air after a rain. These are wise words from such a small girl. Give thanks to God for providing such bountiful blessings to behold.

One day as my husband, Bill, was having coffee at the local coffee shop, a homeless man suffering from alcoholism came in and sat down on a chair with his guitar and preformed a song. When he finished playing, he quietly got up and left. He did not ask for money and he bothered no one. He performed for the love of it. Bill said the guy had a huge smile on his face as he performed, and Bill recognized that each one of us has a talent; we just need to discover what it is. Embrace you talent—if you keep your talent buried everyone loses.

Start thinking of your challenges as blessings, because maybe if you stop for a moment you will decide that whatever has been challenging is a message to make changes, to eliminate an activity from your life, to let go or change direction. How often, after we have been through a taxing time in our lives, do we recognize the learnings or blessings we received as a result of what we endured? During this new encounter try remembering your previous learnings.

There are some incidences that are not blessings, of course, but the discoveries and accomplishments that came out of them are. When my infant son died it was a devastating experience, and one day I found a random quote that eased my pain: "His job here on earth is done." Many times throughout the years those words brought comfort to me when I thought about my child, and the experience motivated me to start cleaning up my life, which eventually led to working in the social-service sector. When I was employed as a Victim Services practitioner I encountered numerous death-related incidents, and I tried to make sense of why the young and innocent died and those performing acts of violence often did not, and I would recall the phrase "His job here on earth is done," which once again comforted me. I have no idea what the bigger picture is, but finding a new way to look at some of life's hardships is essential to survival.

Many people who have endured great anguish have refocused their energy into creating movements for change, like Mothers Against Drunk Driving or people like the Cadmans. Chuck and Donna Cadman's sixteen-year-old son, Jesse, was stabbed to death in a random street attack by a group of young people on October 18, 1992. The Cadmans created the group Crime Responsibility and Youth (CRY), and counseled teens who were likely to become violent. Chuck Cadman also campaigned for stronger laws regarding the Young Offenders Act. He entered politics as a result of his involvement in combating youth violence and has continued to combat it, and to fight for victims' rights. Cadman was elected to Canadian Parliament and successfully raised the maximum jail term for parents whose children commit crimes while under their supervision.

Similarly, John and Reve Walsh's six-year-old son was abducted and murdered in 1981. John Walsh is known as the former host of *America's Most Wanted*, but he also worked as an anti-crime activist. The Walsh family founded the Adam Walsh Child Resource Center, a nonprofit organization dedicated to legislative reform. Their efforts led to the creation of the Missing Children Act of 1982 and the Missing Children's Assistance Act of 1984. Walsh continues to testify before Congress and state legislatures on crime, missing children, and victims'-rights issues. It is important to find ways to cherish the life and memory of those we love without losing ourselves in the anguish.

It is important to give and to receive, but balance is also essential. If you tend to be a giver, are you also open to receiving those same kind words and deeds that you provide to others? Often givers do not know how to receive, and it is quite simple: just say "thank you" and allow the giving to happen. The reason burnout is dominant in the helping sectors is because wonderful giving people often end up giving too much of themselves and lose the mind-body-spirit connection. Iyanla Vanzant, author and spiritual leader, said, "You can only give from your overflow; your cup must be full first." If you are giving from less than a full cup, it will go empty and then you are unable to help others which may be very difficult to even recognize yourself. At the same time, too much "self-care" can be a tactic for avoiding participation in activities that require our attention. Life is all about balance, and God wants you to be filled with the spirit because then you can do great work for others and yourself all in His name; be God-centered, not self-centered. God is love, and love lives to give, not lives to get.

The acts of giving and receiving should not be underestimated; see how it changes your outlook regarding your own circumstances. When you give, you also get— it comes full circle. The outward act of giving creates an inward feeling of joy. You can change someone's day by acknowledging the good service you received or by providing a smile or a helping hand. It costs nothing, but you and the recipient of your kind acts gain richness of spirit. Grateful people are happy people, and the spirit of gratefulness keeps you, your home, your community, and your nation alive. Make it a practice not to leave kind words unsaid or unacknowledged.

Children

"While we try to teach our children all about life, our children teach us what life is all about."

—Angela Schwindt

During the writing of this book, I consulted many experts and drew from the experiences of the experts in my life. Some of those experts are children. Children are born heart-conscious and their child mind is trustful, pure, imaginative, and open. As a child we laugh at silliness, like farts and burps. We imagine we are Superman and Cinderella. We love to explore our world, whether it is in the backyard or the community. We play in the sandbox with children from various races, economic status, religions, and cultures. There is no fear and no judgment passed. We give love unconditionally to our parents, siblings, and pets. A baby has the ability to make everyone smile. As we grow we are told what to be afraid of or that we are different, which is supposed to be a negative thing. We learn to stop using our imagination, and stop laughing at silliness, and we develop limited trust. We learn that we must grow up, but often the message that we need to leave behind our childish ways but keep our pure hearts is lost.

The school curriculum has changed since I attended, and much of it has changed for the better. Children now discuss current world events in the classroom. When I attended school we discussed the Queen's visit to Canada or an eclipse of the moon—basically rare occurrences. I can have thought-provoking discussions with children about politics, the environment, religion, law, and order. What I find fascinating is their ability to take something that appears very complicated and provide very realistic and simple solutions. Often I have better conversations with children about these issues than with adults. Children hear about world events from television and the Internet; they are no longer isolated from the world in the way that maybe they once were. You may think that children should not be discussing such heavy topics, but I think we need to be asking children for the answers. For generations we have been making decisions without any consideration of the impact on the generations to follow, and they are left with our messes to deal with. If we consulted children we would be able to create a heart-conscious world.

My niece Kaitlyn read the book *Three Cups of Tea*, by Greg Mortenson and David Oliver Relin, as part of the curriculum in her seventh-grade class and shared her insights with me. The book is the story of Mortenson, his journey in Pakistan, and his mission to build schools in the region. He encountered many challenges, but he successfully built thirty schools. What impacted Kaitlyn was the children of Pakistan and what they had to do to live because, as she said, "It was a very harsh life." Kaitlyn said that the children wanted to attend school and they helped to build the schools; she was in awe because in her community, to the best of her knowledge, most children did not want to go to school and they most certainly would not have helped build one.

The Pakistani children were given fat from the hides of the animals that were killed, and the fat was like candy for them. The boys were taken on hunting expeditions to learn how to get food for the family, and although they went out hunting, it did not mean that they would return successful. Kaitlyn gained an appreciation for the food she has available to her, and she recognized the importance of not wasting it. The girls in very remote communities appeared to be treated with less respect than in other areas, and Kaitlyn recognized the unfairness of it.

Kaitlyn had a lot of compassion for the children because living in the middle of a war zone was not their fault. As a result of reading the book, she decided that she wanted to raise funds to provide the children of Pakistan with school supplies. She and a classmate set up a table at the locale cafe and asked for donations for the project and each contributor was given a cookie that Kaitlyn baked and a detailed flyer outlining the living conditions and what the proceeds would be used for. One penny in Pakistan can buy a child a pencil, and if a child is given twelve dollars, he can go to school for one year.

During the time of the fund-raising campaign there was news coverage of Mortenson being accused of taking money from the project. I asked Kaitlyn for her thoughts, and she said that if Greg Mortenson did take the money, it was his decision and she could not do anything about it. She believed that regardless of the accusations, Mortenson did some good work by opening schools and she would not allow it to affect her efforts to support children in need. The money raised was given to the Central Asia Institute, and as a result of her campaign, Kaitlyn opened the minds and hearts of many strangers that entered the cafe that day. When people reviewed the cost of supplies, they were in amazement and realized they had no need to complain about their situation. Some stated they held judgments about giving to individuals in other parts of the world, but were now reconsidering.

The reason I shared this story is not only because I am proud of Kaitlyn, but also because she represents how children are able to see the heart of a matter. With their innocence and limited vocabulary, children are able to cut to the core of an issue. Kaitlyn not only had compassion, but she also acted on her concerns. She did not allow the negative attention that Mortensen was receiving to interfere with her mission and she demonstrated how an open heart can touch the lives of many individuals.

If you have children or grandchildren or nieces and nephews, I encourage you to let them lead the way from time to time so you can remember and experience the wonders of the world from their viewpoint. Children can be the teachers, and if we follow their heart-conscious lead we can change the world. Use your imagination to envision a world from a child's heart-conscious position, and then act on your vision. The future is our children, and our children are love.

Chapter Review:

- When you wake up, shout with gusto, "I am alive!"

- For one day play the child's game of I spy "blessings" and keep track of how many you find. I spy _____ blessing and keep track.

- Find reasons to smile.

- See the world through the eyes of a child.

- Repeat all the steps over and over again.

- Add photos of blessings to your toolbox.

⁊ 7 ⁊

From Fear to Freedom

The Lord's Prayer

Our Father, who art in heaven,
hallowed by thy name.
Thy kingdom come,
thy will be done
on earth as it is in heaven.
Give us this day our daily bread;
and forgive us our trespasses,
as we forgive them that trespass against us.
And lead us not into temptation,
but deliver us from evil:
for thine is the kingdom and the power and the glory,
for ever and ever.
Amen.

"So do not fear, for I am with you; do not be dismayed, for
I am your God. I strengthen you and help you; I will uphold
you with my righteous hand."

—Isaiah 41:10 (NIV)

FEAR HOLDS US BACK from living life to the fullest. When we were children we seemed fearless; we rode our bicycles with gusto, jumping them over any object we could locate, and we chased each other with sticks and were free to roam the community, exploring. Some fears were instilled at an early age by adults due to concern for our safety: do not touch the hot stove or do not put your sister's dirty socks in your mouth. Some homes and neighborhoods were physically and verbally violent. Therefore, many fears were instilled. As we became adults we forgot to leave the fears behind. Each time we turn on the television, it seems there are more reasons to be afraid. We developed some important safety devices and rules, like seatbelts and no drinking and driving, but it does not appear that our fears have lessened—they may have actually increased, and the biggest fear is *fear of self*.

Rachael was a brilliant young client and seemed to intellectually grasp all the material presented during the life-skills course, but she struggled with implementing the information. She consumed books and wrote beautiful poetry expressing her feelings and views, but there was always something missing. Many people saw Rachael's potential and told her how special she was, but she failed to see it herself.

She went on to college and took one course after another. She often changed her career aspirations partway through a course and would take classes on a new topic. She was always on a quest for knowledge, but there seemed to be something lacking. Rachael took classes on physiology, reflexology, environmental studies, etc. She never completed a degree program and seemed to always be looking for her next educational fix. She was concerned about appearing dumb, so she specialized in taking an assortment of courses to be able to converse on a variety of topics, but because she never obtained her degree, she always felt beneath others. Rachael became an expert at self-sabotage.

Many years after Rachael completed the life-skills program, she contacted me to discuss why she was stuck. We discussed spirit, and again she seemed to intellectually understand the information but could not release herself from fear. The fear was familiar and comfortable and, although a potentially better future lay before her, she was unable to trust. Rachael would give me countless examples of how she was letting a higher source into her life; she described messages she received, but in the next breath would describe a detailed plan for how to achieve the outcome she desired—because, she reminded me, she had Free Will. Every time she said *Free Will*, I could hear the determined tone, telling me that nothing and no one was going to tell her what to do. What Rachael failed to see was that when you relinquish to God, you become free. There is no fear and your path becomes smooth as long as you get out of the way and let God be.

The stumbling we face is of our own making; we become fearful and get in the way. God is about possibilities; we interfere because we need to be in control, and we create impossibilities! Utilizing counseling services and alternative healing services to reveal your fears, why they were created, and where you are blocked is imperative, but ultimately it is your choice to remove them.

A nationwide survey conducted by R.H. Bruskin Associates, (1973) stated that most people would rather die instead of speak publically. Death is second on the list. Review what you are afraid of: is it a realistic or unrealistic fear? Would you actually die from public speaking or from seeing a spider? Your mind-body is unable to distinguish between real and imagined dangers, so when you focus on unrealistic dangers your body provides the same adrenaline rush as you would need when running from a wild animal. When someone is holding a gun to your head it is realistic to be afraid. Almost one hundred percent of the time when I explored fears with clients, the fears were based on unrealistic dangers, and the biggest was the fear of the unknown: "She/he will leave me," "I'm not good enough," "I will be poor," "I will fail," and so on.

We create crazy-making thinking and behaviors. If you fear loss of independence and are concerned that you will end up living in the basement apartment of your child's home when you become a senior citizen but you are now only thirty-five years old, you are giving way too much time and energy to the unknown. Even if you are sixty-five and you have these concerns, you are still missing the opportunity to live in the now. We dedicate a tremendous amount of time and energy to worrying about things no one has any control over. When all your time is spent stressing about the future, you miss many opportunities and joys in the present. Fear suffocates and blocks the spirit.

What blocks are you experiencing? Create a fear checklist and determine what fears are realistic and unrealistic. Once you identify your fears, change the CD playing in your mind or use the meditation exercise in Chapter 4, "Forgiveness."

One night when I was having a nightmare I started to recite the Lord's Prayer, and the nightmare immediately stopped and I felt at peace. I have since recited it during fearful times, and every time I do, I get the same immediate and peaceful effect. When we take a moment to recite a positive and uplifting scripture, poem, quote, or prayer, we create a shift in our mind, driving out fear. Just imagine the impact it would have on the world if we did this when we faced something or someone we did not understand or feared.

One day a discussion about Hitler was taking place and I said the whole process was fascinating to me because Hitler could have been viewed like a crazy guy on the street uttering nonsense, but large masses of people bought what he was selling, which resulted in massive human destruction. Immediately following the discussion a ten-year-old girl asked me how discrimination got started and she used segregation as an example. I provided examples of power and control, and belief systems, and finally I said, "It is all about fear." When we are not familiar or are uncomfortable regarding people and things we do not understand, fears are created, and when fears go unchecked it can lead to discrimination. She said, "It is like bullying, but on a big worldwide level." Out of the mouths of babes great wisdom is revealed; child wisdom is so profound because children allow themselves to voice what comes to their heart and mind. They do not censor themselves likes adults often do.

For everything there is an opposite: light-darkness, yin-yang, hot-cold, sunshine-rain, praise-criticism and love-fear. Know that when you are coming from a fear-based place you cannot come from a love base. Each time you eliminate a fear, you replace it with love. Often I see the first stumbling block to change is the fear to look within. Going inside is not easy; it is like when you were a child exploring the closet with the belief that monsters lived there. The monsters inside of your being were created from your experiences and beliefs about yourself. Some of those messages may have been instilled by others, but ultimately you choose how you respond and what monsters you want to keep. As you would tell a child, we need to get a light and shine it in the closet to reveal there is nothing to be afraid of. Love is the light and God is love, so when you fully invite God to assist, the monsters disappear.

My father was hospitalized in September 2009 due to another heart attack, and this time he was informed the medical staff could not perform any more "miracles" to keep him alive because his body was too weak; it was time to consider a Do Not Resuscitate order. It was a wake-up call for him because he prided himself on disobeying doctors' orders and proving he was tougher than they gave him credit for. He glowed each time the doctor reviewed his medical history and said, "You are a miracle because with all that is medically wrong with you, you should be dead." Dad did not view his life as precious gift, but as one more time he one-upped the medical profession and, I think, God.

In the following weeks, Dad struggled to follow the doctors' instructions, and he did better than before, but his health continued to fail and a month later he was back in the hospital. It was obvious that Dad was much closer to death. My father always said that he believed in God, but he was not a religious man and his actions over the years definitely indicated he was not embracing any kinship to God. In his early days my Dad lived a rough life, but he softened over time. My sister and her children had been praying that Dad would accept Jesus into his life, especially as he grew closer to death. I waited for my Dad to gather us around to make amends for any pain he caused, *sorry* had never been in his vocabulary. As the days grew closer to his death, my sister and I did not see the results we had been hoping for. What I was beginning to realize was that the man I always saw as tough, rugged, and tell-it-as-it-is was very, very afraid. My father was afraid of death and for once in his life he could not use his voice. He loved to talk, but his voice had become weak due to the illness. The illness could not be blamed for the loss of his voice, though; it had become frozen in fear.

One night, I entered Dad's hospital room to discuss his fears surrounding death. I told him that there was nothing to be afraid of and he would be going to heaven because God loved him. I told Dad that whatever he imagined heaven to be, he could create, and since he loved Percheron draft horses there would be horses waiting for him. I told him that if he wished to fight to live, I supported him, but if he wanted to journey to the other side, I also supported him—it was his choice. I reminded

Dad that God loved him; all was well with God and there were no unresolved issues on earth that needed addressing. Dad said, "Beautiful words," and he thanked me and I left him to rest.

The next morning my mother and I arrived early to meet with the doctors and I stopped in my tracks as I entered the hospital room because the change in my father was dramatic. He was completely into his journey home to the Lord. The nursing staff asked us to gather the family together and palliative care would be provided in the hospital because he was too weak to transfer to the specialized unit. Dad labored for breath throughout the day—he was unable to communicate and was basically nonfunctional—but at one point he raised himself up and with an outstretched arm and with a big smile on his face, he said, "Jesus, I saw," and he laid back on the bed. My father adored all of his grandchildren and I believe he delivered this final message to let them know their prayers had been answered, which brought tremendous comfort. Dad remained with us until the following day, and as I watched him take his last few breaths, I watched the wrinkles disappear. He looked twenty years younger, and he glowed and smiled. Dad died on October 20, 2009, at 8:05 p.m.

Dad gave me a precious gift: the opportunity to be with him when he transitioned from life to death. Previous to this experience I did not have a fear of death, but he provided confirmation that there is nothing to fear and he proved to me that Jesus and the spiritual realm are real.

A man who was, basically, a nonbeliever was met by Jesus to be guided home. For me the message was clear.

I encourage you to start living now, and do not wait until you are ill or on your deathbed. Do not be dead while alive; life can be incredibly joyous when you remove the fears that bind you. God is always waiting with an outstretched hand to welcome you into the love of life.

Chapter Review:

- What fears are holding you back?

- Are your fears realistic or unrealistic?

- Change the CD or use a meditation exercise to overcome your fears.

- Seek professional assistance to overcome any fears you cannot resolve yourself.

- Ask God for help.

☙ 8 ☙

Letting Go

"Give It Away"
Performed by George Strait; written by Bill Anderson,
Buddy Cannon and Jamey Johnson

She was stormin' through the house that day
And I could tell she was leavin'
And I thought ah, she'll be back
'Til she turned around and pointed at the wall and said
"That picture from our honeymoon, that night in Frisco Bay

"Just give it away," She said, "Give it away"
And that big four-poster king-size bed, where so much love
was made
Just give it away," she said "Just give it away"
Just give it away
There ain't nothin' in this house worth fightin' over
Oh, and we're both tired of fightin' anyway
So just give it away
So I tried to move on
But I found that each woman I held

Just reminded me of that day
When that front door swung wide open, she flung her diamond ring
Said "Give it away, just give it away"
And I said, "Now, honey, don't you even want, your half of everything?"
She said, "Give it away, Just give it away"
Just give it away
There ain't nothin' in this house worth fightin' over
Oh, and we're both tired of fightin' anyway
So just give it away
So I'm still right here where she left me
Along with all the other things
She don't care about anymore.
Like that picture from our honeymoon,
that night in Frisco Bay
She said "Give it away," well, I can't give it away
And that big four-poster king-size bed, where all
our love was made

She said, "Give it away," well, I can't give it away
I've got a furnished house, a diamond ring
And a lonely broken heart full of love
And I can't even give it away

"The Care the Eagle Gives Her Young"
by R. Deane Postlethwaite (1925-1980)

The care the eagle gives her young, safe in her lofty nest,
is like the tender love of God for us made manifest.

As when the time to venture comes,
she stirs them out to flight,
so we are pressed to boldly try to strive for daring height.
And if we flutter helplessly, as fledging eagles fall,
beneath us lift God's mighty wings to bear us, one and all.

"When I let go of what I am, I become what I might be."
—Lao-tzu

WHAT IS LETTING GO all about? It is the release or relinquishment or surrendering or abandonment of all our fears and attachments to belongings, people, places, and characteristics. But how do we let go?

My dear friend Ruth shared with me her story about letting go. Ruth and her husband, Paul, were in extreme financial distress in the 1980s when the interest rates skyrocketed, and they found themselves, like many others did, in a financial vise grip. Ruth had just given birth to their third child and every waking moment was spent trying to figure out how to make the mortgage payment on the farm. No matter how much they trimmed the budget, though, they were unable to get themselves out of debt. One night as Ruth and Paul lay awake in bed reviewing their options and trying to come up with a creative solution, Ruth sat bolt upright with the realization that they have three beautiful children sleeping down the hall, and what more in the world could they ask for? They were very fortunate to have three beautiful and healthy children. As they discussed how blessed they were, the solution to their financial burden became apparent: they would declare bankruptcy. They acknowledged it was not the miracle they had envisioned, but it was the best possible solution given the circumstances. Within a very short time the paperwork was completed and they found a new residence and lived a much richer life because they realized their assets were their children, not the possessions they were trying to hang onto.

In Buddhism desire is likened to poison. With desires you are never free. Food, sex, shopping, gambling, work, drugs, and alcohol all come back again and again. Try to catch a rainbow—it is a useless and impossible task. A rainbow is light and water, and it is always in front of you. You can chase it, but you will never catch it because the light moves; it is an illusion, just like our desires. The rainbow is pretty and the chase is fun, but in the end we will be disappointed. The whole premise of the Bible is about the need to be filled with love versus looking elsewhere for fulfillment. Addictions occur because the spirit is not full and we turn to food, sex, relationships, shopping, gambling, work, drugs, alcohol, etc., to supply what is missing. When we are filled by spirit, there is no void, and when we relinquish everything we gain all.

As children we heard fairytale stories of princesses and knights in shining armor, and often we search for the fairytale when we are adults. A new relationship is exciting and all-consuming; we are "high on love" and are receiving bucketloads of endorphins, and we begin to believe that the other person is all that we need to be complete. When our endorphins return to a normal level and the relationship starts getting real, we decide that it is over or we continue the relationship, recognizing the initial excitement for what it was or not thinking there is something wrong with us. When we try to fill ourselves from outside sources we are grasping for pleasure from others, and attachment is developed and problems are created.

Often clients would ask if they had *victim* written on their forehead in neon letters, and I would tell them it might as well be because their body language and entire being screamed *victim*, and an abuser could spot them from across the room, which was why they were drawn to each other. Many people told me that the "bad boys" and "bad girls" were fun, and when they tried dating the regular guy or girl, it was boring. The translation is, "I can be loved only when I am being abused," "The regular guy/girl will discover I am not worthy," or "This is familiar, and therefore safe." I would tell clients if they wanted a partner they needed to stop looking, focus on their own health, and once they were healthy they would realize they did not need a partner, but if a partner happened to come along it would be a bonus versus the main event. Many clients who observed this method are living very happy and peaceful lives with partners they no longer consider boring, but rather safe and loving. Once you are connected mind-body-spirit, anything or anyone that comes into your life is special and adds to your life in the overflow because you are already filled.

In Colette Baron-Reid's book *The Map*, she has a wonderful exercise on letting go. Basically, the exercise has you list seven attachments, number them in order of importance, and do it quickly so it is instinctual rather than thought-provoking. Ensure you give yourself privacy and time to fully engage in the activity. Beside the list of attachments, write your feelings. Then go into a meditative state and imagine paradise awaits but there is a large canyon between you and paradise and the only way to get there is by leaving all of your attachments behind. Start releasing each attachment one, by one from the least important to the most important. You may have strong emotional and physical reactions because your mind and body do not know that this is an exercise. Allow yourself to fully feel each release. When you have released all of your attachments, you will be met by a loving spiritual guide who will take your hand, tell you that you were brave, and fly with you over the canyon. When you reach paradise you see everything you let go of is there waiting for you. You never lost the attachments because they were never yours to begin with. After the exercise, pamper yourself by having a soak in the tub, and try journaling your experiences.

When I did this exercise I found it very powerful. When I reflected I was surprised at what did not make it on the list, like friends. As I released the attachments I felt my emotions very strongly and it was as if I were actually saying goodbye forever to precious people, possessions, and characteristics. Due to the nature of my work, I found it very easy to release most things. At one point in my career I dealt with house fires, so I had given some consideration to what was important, and when dealing with sudden death I also knew I would survive because, after all, my clients find ways to carry on. What challenged me the most was the loss of wisdom. I believed that if I had wisdom I could get through all loss, but I had to now face losing it.

I visualized having Alzheimer's disease; I would not know I had lost anything, I would be happy, and I was finally able to let go of wisdom. I felt the spirit guide hold my hand as we flew off over a canyon, and I realized we always have spiritual support in life, but this time I was completely aware. I knew God was always with me. His love never disappears. His love never fails. I felt, "I am love, I love, and I am whole and complete." Everything I was attached to was not me, so nothing could ever be taken from me. There was nothing to lose because nothing belongs to me.

The reason we are looking at attachment is not because you are required to lack money, fame, material possessions, or relationships, but when you are attached to these things it is easy to get confused and believe all of it is of your own making and God is not needed, so why would you want to let go? If this is your belief then releasing may seem like a void will be created; however, the attachments will not provide a straight line to eternal life—it can be achieved only by love, and God is love. Give some thought to how important a person or object is. Everything will end someday; people die and things break, but when you have the love of God, money, fame, material possessions, and relationships will not have a grip on you, and you will be prosperous in all ways. When you let go and let God, all things are possible!

Ego is an intangible mental occurrence, and the ego gains strength through attachment, desire, anger, and hatred. The ego needs activity in order to exist, and attachments, anger, and greed are the obvious activities of the ego. The more yearnings and dislikes we have, the more the ego seems to flourish. The ego and yearnings depend on each other for survival. It is like your car; when you fill it with gas it can go for many miles, but when you stop refilling the tank, the warning light will start flashing and eventually the car will stop. Since the ego is an illusion, its yearnings cannot be satisfied. It is like having a hole in the gas tank and the objects we yearn for are an excuse for the ego to flash for attention—for more gas—and we create justifications for more road trips. There are yard or garage sales, attics, closets, and storage units full of things unused, primarily thanks to ego. There are now many television shows dedicated to people's search for treasures in these various places. When my husband and I sold our home we downsized, but still put belongings into a storage unit and moved into a six-meter (twenty-foot) travel trailer for the summer. We never missed any the belongings in the storage unit and we had to re-evaluate why we had so much stuff. Do not rush to give all your possessions away or purposely create hardships for yourself. The requirements of daily living still must be fulfilled. Explore your heart and discern what is right for you.

The ego also seems very alive when we get upset, irritated, and angry at others for small things, but it causes a lot of suffering. We can get an energy buzz from some of these small irritants and upsets, which can lead to a life filled with drama but no real substance. I encourage you to give your ego a name like Joe or Sally, and when ego appears greet him or her either verbally or mentally. Say, "Hello, Joe. I am not surprised to see you." The ego loses some of its power when you acknowledge it. Ego likes to make trouble behind the scenes in the dark, and when you shed light on ego it tends to fade and will eventually disappear. But remember that ego is always lurking in the shadows waiting for an opportunity to appear. As you become familiar with greeting your ego it will bring a smile to your face.

Twyla was a client who fully understood the need to let go. She was a single parent with an ex-spouse who refused to pay child support; she was operating her own business and volunteering for school functions and attending to the emotional hurts of her children when their father used them as his sounding board for perceived grievances he had with Twyla. Twyla put her needs last for many years. She struggled to keep positive and meet all the demands of life. One day she decided it was time to start living rather than living to exist. She said, "I had been sitting around waiting for a miracle, but discovered I needed to take action."

Twyla knew she needed to let go of the expectation of child support and that her continued battle to obtain money from her ex-spouse was her ego pushing her. His lack of responsibility in supporting their children was unjust, but she had become bitter, and it prevented her from moving forward. Although there was a court order, Twyla knew he would never pay the child support. She decided to move during the summer school break to a community where there was family support and many more educational opportunities for the children and her. Twyla understood that when she was trying to control the outcomes in her life, the need to control was actually controlling her.

Once she released control Twyla started to see the many choices in front of her. At the same time she remained flexible and knew the move might not be permanent. She was taking life one day at a time and not placing herself in a gridlock position. Twyla recognized fixed plans led to struggles because she would be trying to implement the plan and she might lose sight of possibilities and opportunities along the way. When she relinquished the need to have control, she was set free. There were times of stress—especially when her teenage children were reluctant to move to a new community—but she returned to her original intent and found peace.

Twyla approached challenges with an open mind and heart; she looked at struggles as blessings to new insights. Other people constantly asked for a detailed plan, which she did not have, and she knew it was transference of their fears. Twyla remained strong in her faith. She was willing to accept whatever the outcome may be because there was a larger purpose at work, which she was unable to see at the current moment, but she trusted the plan would eventually be revealed to her. Twyla sold many of her belongings, closed her business, prepared to leave town, and remained open to possibilities; she now glows.

Twyla is a shining example of the fact that when you let go of fears and attachments you begin to see and hear the messages surrounding you. Moving to a new community is not always the answer; you must discern what is right for you. Many of my clients believed moving was the only solution, but when you relinquish fears and attachments you see multiple solutions. If you remain attached to your baggage it will go with you and interfere with your new surroundings, just like a turtle packs its shell everywhere it goes.

Change is sometimes uncomfortable for you and those around you, but it is necessary and it is constant. When participants in the life-skills program attend group they are told it is not a place to make friendships. If at the end of the course a friendship is established, then it is a bonus. Each individual comes to group with some sort of baggage, and as time goes on, they begin to leave the baggage behind. But each person will assess her own pace; if participants try to develop friendships early in the program, it could lead to discord because each person is moving at a different pace, plus it is important to focus on their own needs for the time being and not be distracted by others.

As you create change, your family and friends may not be as supportive as you would anticipate. You have established roles and patterns with each other, and once you start to shift and change the established order the other people's fears come charging in because they no longer know where they fit. There may come a time when you must discern whether you keep some relationships or change the frequency of contact because it is detrimental to your health to do otherwise.

Some people appear to have everything they want and are cozy with contentment. They need nothing and no one, but actually they are miserable. If they really looked at themselves they would see poverty because real wealth is having a relationship with yourself and others, and being clothed in garments of love. God works through relationships and

He is always waiting to be invited to reveal the abundance that engulfs you so true wealth can be enjoyed.

Remez Sasson, author, creator and owner of the website SuccessConsciousness.com said, "All techniques and methods of inner development have a common goal. They all aim toward freedom and enlightenment." A technique for release I used with clients was to have them blow all their fears and attachments into a balloon and write on the balloon their feelings or yearnings or the name of a person or possession that needed to be let go, and the clients would let the wind carry the balloon away to God with a prayer of thanks to God for taking the burden.

As you struggle to let go, remember that God is there and invite Him to help you release, and if you flutter and feel helpless, know that God is there to lift you up. Remember as you release or relinquish or surrender, you are loved, and by relinquishing your fears and attachments you allow love to fill your being. When you are on your death bed you are unable to take your possessions with you, but in the end those things do not matter. At the end of life, no one ever wishes they had worked more. The only assurance in life is God's love for you: it remains forever.

Chapter Review:

- What are you attached to?

- Choose an exercise to release your attachment.

- Repeat the exercises as many times as needed to release all of your attachments.

- Add balloons and a felt pen to your toolbox.

∞ 9 ∞

Faith

"Faith, While Trees Are Still in Blossom"
by Fred Kaan© 1976 Hope Publishing Company

Faith, while tress are still in blossom,
plans the picking of the fruit,
faith can feel the thrill of harvest
when the buds begin to sprout.

Long before the dawn is breaking,
faith anticipates the sun.
Faith is eager for the daylight,
for the work that must be done.

Long before the rains were coming,
Noah went and built an ark.
Abraham, the lonely migrant,
saw the light beyond the dark.

Faith, uplifted, tamed the water of the undivided sea,
and the people of the Hebrews

found the path that made them free.
Faith believes that God is faithful:
God will be what will be!
Faith accepts the call, responding,
"I am willing, Lord, send me."

"The way to see faith is to shut the eye of reason."
—Benjamin Franklin

BY NOW YOU ARE wondering, What does all this have to do with God answering prayers? It is like when the monks covered the golden Buddha to protect it from soldiers; we too have covered ourselves for protection. Throughout the years we have been hurt physically and emotionally by others or we hurt ourselves, and consequently we created a coating to protect ourselves from the pain. The golden Buddha was uncovered, and now it is our job to uncover our essence and we need to go back to the beginning to unravel the ties that bind us.

When we were children, we quickly learned words hurt us, so we need to become aware of what started the corrosion. Over time, we forget how much fun it was to run, play, sing, dance, laugh, rest, and be in nature, so we need to be reminded. As an infant, letting go was easy because if someone showed us something different we would drop one thing like a hot potato and reach for the new thing. As a child, forgiveness was not difficult; we could be mad at our playmate one minute and playing together again the next. But as time went on, forgiving and letting go became more challenging; the power of hurtful words and actions was already taking effect. Our core is no different than it was from birth, and once we chisel the mud off, we see what has been waiting there along.

To be able to hear God's answers to our prayers we need to be able to hear with our mind-body-spirit. God speaks to us in many forms; we may hear a voice, have a feeling, hear a song, dream, have a sense of knowing or a hunch, feel intuition, have a flash thought, or see a bumper sticker, but if we are bound up with all these other issues, we cannot hear, feel or see the answers He is giving us. Sometimes when you drive your car you end up at your destination without ever seeing the scenery along the way, because the route is repetitive and you are acting on autopilot. You missed the new blossoms on the trees or the road sign informing you of a shortcut, and just maybe those were the messages you needed, but you were unconscious to what was being presented to you.

Faith in God is trust and knowing He is real, even though we can't see Him. Even if you do not believe in God, having faith is having the confidence to believe the present and future will work as they are supposed to. I have no idea how a fax or an email works. I am amazed that when I put the paper in the machine or type words on my computer and hit Send, within seconds someone can read what I just entered. When I hit Send, like my prayers, my fax or email goes into the unknown, but I trust everything will work as it designed to.

You do not need a life plan, but if you have one that is okay; the important thing is not to be attached to the plan and to be flexible, not orchestrating the steps and outcome. Faith is also like driving in the dark with the headlights on. When you drive in the dark you can see only a few meters (feet) in front of you, where the light is projected. You trust that the road will continue and all will be well. If the road is unfamiliar and there are many twists and curves in the road you do not pull over to the side of the road and wait until it becomes daylight. You may reduce your speed and proceed with caution, but you trust that the road will take you to your destination. You also believe the vehicle you are traveling in will get you to your destination because you have performed all the necessary maintenance.

There is a map for the road called your life, but like the car you must trust that God provided the equipment to get you to your destination; trusting God as He leads you a few steps at a time. When you encounter challenges (twists and curves), it is an opportunity to slow down and discern the road you are traveling, because if you miss the exit ramp to paradise, you must continue to drive until you can find a turnaround spot, or forge ahead looking for another exit ramp that will lead you to the same spot. God gave you Free Will and you can ignore His road signs just like you ignore your car's GPS, but you are responsible for the choices you make.

Living consciously is living in the moment, which allows you the freedom to make decisions and choices based on what is being presented to you at the time. When we get stuck on our planned life or what society tells us life is supposed to look like, we miss the exciting desserts before our eyes. The general rule of society is to get a good education, develop a career, marry, buy a house, have children, and save money to enjoy retirement in a comfortable fashion. This is the formula for a successful life. All of these things are fabulous, and if you have them or want them, the key is to be doing those things consciously, not on autopilot because society says so.

Throughout my career I noticed the difference between people with faith and those without. When horrific situations occurred the people with faith seemed more resilient, but the people without faith had no hope and it was extremely challenging to assist those individuals to move forward; they often got stuck in victimization.

Faith is also about action. You can believe that life will improve and wait for change to occur, or you can begin to make changes and witness your life changing. This is where people get confused about how *they* made things better, not how *God* made things better, and this is the reason they believe they do not need God. I read a story about a man who prayed to God to win the lottery and every Friday night he sat by the telephone waiting for it to ring with the news of his win. After many years went by, he called out to God, "Why have you not answered my prayers?" God replied, "You need to buy a lottery ticket." The story illustrates that we are partners with God in this journey called life.

Many people tell me they must stay at a job they dislike immensely because of the pension plan, and when I inquire about their retirement date, I hear "Oh, in ten or eleven years." Wow! How sad is that? We spend the majority of our adult life working and being miserable; now that is hell. Consider the low endorphin levels when you work at something you despise, and the toll it takes on your mind-body-spirit. No one knows how much time she has on earth; it is important to be joyous while you are here.

You may be thinking that being unhappy at work is just a part of life and we all need to do things we dislike, like cleaning the house, so how is this any different? When you take an inventory of your life, are you living for yourself or for others? If you have a spouse and children, how are they being impacted by your unhappiness? If you want to make changes, talk with your family and discuss the implications the change may have. As a unit decide how you will be fulfilled mind-body-spirit. You may be surprised at what you learn from one another once you really listen to each other. Single people tell me that they would quit their job they dislike, if only they had a partner to provide support. Well, folks you do, and it is God. You can create all the excuses you want, but the bottom line is action needs to be taken and fear is holding you back. By not taking action, you continue to create a grievance story.

When I discuss faith and taking action with people, I notice the immediate response is to start creating a detailed logic-driven plan. When I tell them that is not faith, but rather control and fear, it is difficult for them to comprehend because we are conditioned to respond in this manner. Remember Rachael, the client who changed majors repeatedly? She said she understood faith, and took a "leap of faith" by setting goals; she created plans to achieve her goals, and was determined that because she had Free Will and could change the course and outcome of her activities at any time. This is not "faith-leaping"—it is fear and control. Faith, like love, is not a tangible object that can be held or seen; it is a knowing. Faith is active because it is love. It is a perfect balance of feeling and action. Preaching is an outward action of inward feelings of love of truth. Kindness is an outward expression of feelings of compassion. Rachael had inward feelings of fear and an outward expression of control.

I was one of those individuals unhappy with my career; I was burnt out from the social-service sector. I knew I needed to make changes, but I was lost as to what type of work I would do next because my career had been dedicated to helping others and I felt so drained that I could not imagine being surrounded by people. I was also the sole income-earner because my husband had been injured in a work accident years earlier and was unable to work. Financially we were in extreme debt because we had been living the lifestyle of two full-time incomes. We were living paycheck to paycheck and the credit-card debt was mounting, plus we were battling with insurance companies over the accident. I felt like a prisoner of circumstances.

My ongoing internal battle was that if I left my job, how could we meet our financial obligations, plus my husband was already feeling low because he could not contribute financially and had limited mobility, thus reducing his ability to perform routine tasks, and I did not want to add to his load. My husband told me that he would support whatever decision I made, but I was concerned he could verbally say he supported me, but then perhaps not emotionally fully support the choice. I was also feeling guilty about the credit-card debt because it was created mostly from my pride because I continued to spend the same as when we had two incomes because I did not want our friends and family to know we were struggling financially. I was also trying to fill the internal void by shopping.

I had a belief in God throughout my life and I periodically practiced prayer and I thought I had faith, but I was discovering that I really knew nothing at all. I started to give a lot of time and attention to eliminating the corrosion in my life to be able to allow my spirit to shine consistently. I had been doing self-healing work for years and I was a firm believer that if you teach it you need to live it. I continued to see a counselor periodically throughout my career because I wanted to ensure that any unresolved issues I had were not transferred to clients. What I lacked was the understanding of the mind-body-spirit connection. I often focused on each one separately, but never concentrated on holistic healing.

One Saturday morning as I entered my office and set my briefcase down, I had an internal knowing—I was finished as a Victim Services practitioner. I also realized having faith was action-based. I sensed immediate and incredible peace. I no longer had any worries or fears. I was completely calm. I had faith in my decision because of the calmness. I was taking a leap of faith. It reminded me of the time I bungee-jumped, but this time I had no ropes attached; I was jumping into the unknown with a belief that God was with me and all would be well. When I shared this knowing with my husband and we discussed the implications my resignation would have on our finances, we knew that we needed to sell our home. I knew my husband supported me emotionally, but the strange thing was that by deciding to resign, I no longer tied my emotional well-being to him: his support was an added bonus. Hours after making the decision to quit, I realized we had equity in our home and the sale of the house would cover most of our debt. This was not something I could see when I was bound with worries; it was only when I took a leap of faith that everything became clear. It is like when you look for something in the cupboard and can't find it but it was in front of your eyes the entire time, or you lose your keys and you search and search and can't find them, but once you stop thinking about the lost keys you locate them.

The next difficult step is to maintain faith to allow God to work with you. When I resigned, I was at the end of my contract and I was fully aware the financial well could go dry immediately, but I trusted God because my decision provided immense peace. When my employers received my letter of resignation, they asked me if I would reconsider if they could obtain adequate funding to change my job description and hire more staff. I agreed to the plan and began writing a proposal for funding, but I was not attached to the outcome. We continued with our decision to sell our home. The funding plan was not guaranteed, but the work provided continued finances while our home was being prepared for sale. If the proposal was successful our debt load would be reduced because we would have sold our home. We recognized a win-win situation.

As I was writing the proposal for the ideal program for our community, I was also training a volunteer, and teaching made my heart sing. I was having an incredibly joyous time at work. We determined the selling figure for our home from a hymn book at church because it resonated with me. *Voices United Psalm 23—The Lord is My Shepherd* was printed on page 747, so our house listing price was $77,747. We had an offer on our house within one week, but it was lower than we expected, and as we were discussing the offer with the broker I had a flash thought: "The offer will have a 500 in it." Since this one did not, so we refused the offer. As time went on I had a lack-of-faith moment. I asked my husband if we made a mistake refusing the offer and he said, "No, it did not feel right." Within a month we accepted an offer for $77,500.

I wrote my proposal, but once I finished it I knew I did not want to implement it. The proposal was an ideal program for our community, but I was not interested in managing staff. I was still teaching, but I knew my time at the organization was coming to an end because I was back doing client work, which was the exact thing I wanted a break from. I submitted the proposal and as the usual process goes in government, it was sitting on a desk waiting to be read. But because I was not attached to the outcome, I was not upset about my work not being acknowledged, which at one time would have become fodder for days of stress.

As we approached the finalization of the sale of our home, I left my job. We put our belongings into storage, and paid off our mortgage and some other bills. We still had some remaining debt and we moved into our small travel trailer, and I began to appreciate the quiet and simplicity of life. I was happier than I had been in months, and actually in my entire lifetime. I was at peace and I knew all was well in my world. After making the decision to leave my job, which was a leap of faith, I followed the signs or the knowing, which helped me to continue to act. It took commitment to remain faithful during that time, but it was essential.

One of my dear friends shared a story from college, about her friend Donna. Donna was attending college because she believed that God directed her to her chosen profession, but she was short on money. She did not have enough funds to pay her rent. Her friends encouraged her to sell her possessions, which were all in storage, but she refused because she believed a check would arrive in the mailbox. God would provide a check solving her financial woes. Finally, Donna was on the verge of being evicted and her friend came to her and asked if she was ready to sell her possessions, but she held firm that a check would be in the mailbox. One friend asked if she ever thought that God sent *her* to help—that *she* was how God was going to provide. Donna spent the day selling her possessions, and she was able to pay her rent and remain in college, and went onto to excel in her chosen profession. God gave Donna signs and messages along the way, but she did not get the outcome she created in her mind. It is important not to be attached or fixed on what the outcome should be. Being conscious allows you to observe and understand the messages that surround you. Sometimes God says no to the outcome we seek because He is able to see the bigger picture. When you fly in an airplane, as you look down below you see many miles in various directions, but as you get closer to landing the view shrinks and becomes limited. We need to remember that we have a limited view, and trust God with the larger picture because when we follow Him the outcome will be more abundant than we could possibly imagine. It is impossible for our mind to imagine the sequence of events that creates universal connection, but we can trust that because God is love all will be as it should be.

Getting to the stage of acceptance when grieving is difficult and it presents quite a trial for faith, too. Praying for others is a very loving act, but it is important to remember that the person we are praying for is having their own dialogue with God and may need something different than what we are praying for. When we pray for others or ourselves we do not always really know what is needed. Do not get attached to what the outcome must look like. You can simply tell God that you love the person you are praying for and you have no idea what their needs are, but you are asking for God to provide, and the same prayer can be used for yourself. You do not need to be eloquent and long-winded in prayer, but if you have a gift of language, that works too; there is no right or wrong way to pray. Seek assistance by inviting God to help, but remember He knows the bigger picture and there is a difference between need and desire. Can you accept the difference?

One year while at the Calgary Stampede in Alberta I saw a man painting a mural on the outside wall of a building. He was standing on scaffolding; he would walk to one end of the wall to dab a bit of paint, walk to the other side or middle and dab a bit more. I thought the mural would be an abstract because he was not following a method I deemed logical, but I trusted the artist knew what he was doing. Each day as I checked on his progress, he continued to use the same method and I could not see any picture appearing, but I accepted the artist's capability. By day four I started to see an outline and by day five a cowboy-themed picture was evident. The artist knew and saw the bigger picture when I could not. Bad things still happen to good people, and faith is not an insurance policy with God that bad things will not happen in your life, but the key is to trust and accept that the artist of life is God.

What is your intention when you make choices or when you pray? It is important to be clear about your intentions. If you are working or volunteering to "fix" something inside you or to "fix" your parents, it is important you get honest with yourself. Many people want to enter the social service sector to help others because they want to make a difference. Sometimes when I explore their career options further, I find the individual actually wants to enter the sector to "fix" childhood issues or their parents or spouse. If you enter the profession to "fix" yourself you will not be focused on clients, and you will be triggered each time an issue similar to yours arises. If you want to "fix" your parents or spouse, know that it is an impossible task—only they can take those steps. When you are acting with unclear intentions you will not be satisfied with the results; you will be faced with many challenges and struggles along the way. What is your intent when you pray to God, and is it consistent? What is it you want answers to?

I believe if we could control the weather we would mess it up because our mind and body are constantly changing. We often change the thermostat in the car or house to get it "just right" and because of this continuous back-and-forth we create confusion. God knows the eternal map and because we are constantly creating confusing messages it is best for us not to have control of the map, just like the weather, and to put our trust in God. Faith is not scientific or logical, and that, my friend, is the very thorny part of the process. If you struggle with the idea of faith, hold on—you are not alone, and there is great compassion for your questions and confusion. When you have unsatisfactory faith, keep it. Do not be discouraged, because one day more knowledge and awareness will appear.

Psalm 23 (NIV): A Psalm of David

"The Lord is my shepherd, I shall not be in want. He makes me lie down in green pastures, he leads me beside quiet waters, he restores my soul. He guides me in paths of righteousness for his name's sake. Even though I walk through the valley of the shadow of death, I fear no evil, for you are with me; your rod and your staff, they comfort me. You prepare a table before me in the presence of my enemies. You anoint my head with oil; my cup overflows. Surely goodness and love will follow me all the days of my life, and I will dwell in the house of the Lord forever."

Looking for Signs

"All I have seen teaches me to trust the Creator for all I have not seen."

—Ralph Waldo Emerson, American essayist, lecturer, and poet

God will provide information to you in many forms and present it in a manner that connects with all of your senses. Everyone has had an experience of a certain song being played on the radio that seemed to speak directly to them, or been thinking about someone then received a call from that person completely out of the blue—that is God giving us what we need. There is no such thing as coincidence or fate; it is God.

My dear friend Linda told a story about how she was asked by eight people to allow her name to be put forward as a president for the parent-teacher association, but she continued to state that she was not interested. Finally, the current president approached her and asked to put her name forward and she stated she would think about it. She went to her car and asked God to give her a sign and immediately God replied, "I gave you nine." She laughed and returned to the meeting and allowed her name to be put forward. She is now the president of the association.

God will often give us repeated signs or signals because we are not observing or listening. We always have Free Will and He will not force us to move in any one direction; it is our choice. Not listening and refusing the choices He gives us is up to us. There is no need to blame God.

One day my friend Yvette and I were discussing looking for signs and she shared about a time when she was a single mother on welfare. As the end of the month approached, she started to get anxious because she had no food in the cupboard and she worried about how to feed her son. Yvette went to the freezer and it was empty, so she relied upon her sister to help her that day. The following day she returned to the freezer and there were three packages of hamburger in it. She realized the hamburger had been there all along, but she was looking in the freezer with the eyes of poverty.

Often we do not see the messages God provides because we are looking at the world around us with foggy eyes. Our current life circumstances and the experiences from the past interfere with our vision. Faith means reaching into the cupboard even when we cannot see, but the crucial element is to reach out because then the blinders will come off. It reminds me of the hymn *Amazing Grace*: "I once was lost and now I am found, was blind, but now I see."

One night as I was writing this book I could hear my brother-in-law Benjamin's voice as I slept and he was telling me to read the book of Deuteronomy in the Old Testament of the Bible. This was a strange request; we never discussed the Bible and I had no idea what his beliefs were. I asked what part of Deuteronomy, because it was kind of long; I immediately woke with knowing I would find the required scripture when I opened the Bible. I got up and straightaway opened the Bible to Deuteronomy 32:2 (NIV)—"Let my teachings fall like rain and my words descend like dew, like showers on new grass, like abundant rain on tender plants." I knew this was exactly the message I was supposed to receive and when I looked at the clock, I realized that my brother-in-law, who was on the other side of Canada, was at work and the message was from God. I knew the purpose of Benjamin's voice was to ensure that I acted on the message because I most likely would have settled back into sleep otherwise.

July 2011 was a very rainy month in my community and each time I heard the rain, I was excited because teachings would arrive. When it poured, I got really excited because I knew the teachings would be plentiful, which is exactly what happened. I decided to look a little deeper into Deuteronomy 32:2, and I learned it was written by a poet who may have been a prophet but was definitely in a circle of theologians with the same convictions. The words were written to inspire new life and effort in the broken people of Israel. We cannot sink to where God cannot reach us. God is always ready with an outstretched hand to save us and to bring us home. When you receive messages or signs in answer to your questions, act on the information you receive, and the results will be astounding.

Voice of God or Mental Illness

As a professional in the mental-health field, I want to differentiate hearing the voice of God from mental illness. God does not speak constantly; He loves and He would never tell you to harm yourself or others. God is not para-noid and would never send that type of message.

I wrote the following when I was in the stages of burnout:

I can relate to Neale Donald Walsch's book Conversations with God *because when I sit with a pen and paper, I too can have a conversation with God (everyone can) and the answers flow from me. It is in the quiet reflective time that I hear that inner voice. Throughout the day-to-day activities I very rarely hear it, let alone listen to that inner calling. Sometimes I get a jolt to attention, but most times it goes unnoticed. I allow the hustle and bustle of the world to drown out the voice and I wonder how I got into the many messes I call my life.*

One day I wake up, I feel heavy and overwhelmed, and I wonder how I got here, like I did nothing to get myself into this particular situation that just occurred. Then I feel trapped and I call out to God, "Help me," and I ask, "How can I be in this miserable spot? Have I not helped enough people? Have I not been good enough? Why must I suffer? When do I get a break?" All the while if I had stayed connected to that inner voice and spent some time reflecting, meditating, maybe I would not be here crying out. Once again, I pick up the pen and paper and I get my reflective answers, but soon I am crying out again.

I consume books like a drug addict needing a fix. I need a solution and tell myself I must be missing something; I did not absorb the material. I blame the book; it focused on only one part of my life. Another book may have more answers, and I look for another fix. I know . . . this time I will contact a fortune-teller and she will provide the answer. . . . I will talk to my friends and rehash my stories and become philosophical and create new stories. . . . I will buy a lottery ticket. Meditate . . . Ahh . . . calmness. But how long will it last? Until there is a bump in the road or a perceived bump and once again the cycle continues, just like an abusive relationship.

Then I ask myself, Why did I get into this type of work; was it to "fix" my parents? Well, it did not work; they were not fixed. Why develop programs for people to heal domestic violence? Many do not want to leave. My mother didn't. Very few clients want to go within to do the work and to challenge their behaviors and belief systems, and now it seems that includes me. I do all this internal work and I lose my day-to-day battle with sanity because I do not want to be quiet and reflective to hear the inner voice. I am too busy, I am too tired, I am . . .

I sit in an office chair and encourage others to do what I can't or won't do myself. As the mirror quote goes [1 Corinthians 13:12 (NIV)], "Now we see but a poor reflection as in a mirror; then we shall see face to face. Now I know in part; then I shall know fully even as I am fully known." I tell myself that journaling is not my thing, but when I really want to chat with God, I write my questions and He responds.

God has an excellent sense of humor, and I forget that too. Time is the greatest humor of all. The clock was created by man, not by God. Who created that darn thing anyway? God created lights in the sky to serve as signs to mark seasons, days, and years, but that was on the fourth day and he took six to create the world, but how long was that really? He had no watch or calendar because man had not yet invented it. God and man are definitely not harmonized with regards to the issue of time.

God rested on the seventh day, but we try to squeeze every ounce out of it we can. We run in and out of church for our Sunday fix. The express lane is not fast enough; we glare at the person in front of us at the supermarket when they have thirteen items and the posted sign states twelve. We get really frustrated with the clerk if she stops and talks to the customer in the coffee line because it slows the process and we may end up waiting an extra two minutes. We get very upset when the school kids work the evening and weekend shifts at the coffee shop because they do not have the speed and the know-how of the experienced staff. As we run out the door with our drink or return to our table, we complain about the state of the world. We especially complain about those youngsters that have no idea what real work is all about or how lazy our society has become. A perfect example is the Toronto Dominion Bank TV commercial with the two grumpy old men on the bench complaining about the state of the world, and how this new generation requires mobile mortgage specialists and pizza delivered to the door, and they start comparing it to their youth—when they wanted something they had to go out and get it, except for milk, which was delivered to the door and that was good. They look at each other in amazement, realizing it was quite a nice service, but they had forgotten. We forget to acknowledge that youngster behind the counter who was slow making our perfect cup of coffee is at least working and trying to make a go of things in a world that damns them just because of their age.

I remember the act of writing this, but I was blind to the content. I kept the pages and rediscovered them while in the process of moving. I did not reread the pages, but decided I should keep them and tucked them into a container that made it into our travel trailer. When I started working on this chapter of the book, I had a feeling that I should retrieve the pages from the container, and as I read the passage, I was once again reminded of God's awesomeness. At the top of page was written, "Life's Answer—Hey, I'm God—All You Need is Love—Simply Love!" I was too corroded and blinded by burnout to see God answered my cry for help. I missed the message and continued to struggle for a year to make my life better. Once I was still, I was reminded of the pages and was able to see clearly the loving message God provided so long ago.

Even as I reread the passage, I had no idea what the mirror quote meant. As I looked at 1 Corinthians for stimulation, I found 13:12, and I knew that it was preciously linked to the passage I wrote. The entire chapter is about love and faith. Faith has to be at its best when things are at their worst, but that does not make it easy to believe in God. We see in a mirror, dimly. God seeks to reveal Himself to us, but often we cannot see. When we live by faith, hope, and love we are on the path leading to home. Our understanding of God is dim and incomplete; He knows us and loves us because He knows everything. I was unable to comprehend my written outburst with God until I started writing this book, and even now I'm making more discoveries. The wondrous thing about spiritual awakening is the constant progression of wisdom. I encourage you to continue your voyage in the unknown and be open to whatever you discover.

All prayers are of equal importance and there is a lot of help to be given; all you have to do is ask. God is always waiting and eager to assist. He will not force Himself on you and He will not interfere with your Free Will. Jessica a pre-teen from a spiritual workshop I conducted, provided an illustration of Free Will. She said, "Fat is not fun, but God gave me Free Will to allow me to be and look any way I want." Every prayer is heard and answered, although the answer may come in a different form than we expect. The more you look for signs or evidence of trust the more you find! There are times answers can elude you and the more you resist the more it persists. Be still and be silent.

When you have doubt it is because you believe you are separated from God, which is disheartening, but it is impossible to be separated from God—the spirit within you *is* God. Just as your children not being physically near you does not mean you do not carry them with you (you love them and carry the love within your being), God is love, therefore He is within you.

During the writing of this book, I received continuous signs of validation and reassurance, which was quite essential since I was embarking on a new road in my life's journey. I would have flash thoughts or insights, which would send me scurrying for a pen and paper to capture what was being presented. Many times I would make a note and have no idea how it would fit into the book, but I kept jotting down information as it came. As I wrote, the short notations turned into deeper thoughts, which made it into the book. There were times I would review the notes and want to cross them off the pad because I could not see how they could possibly fit, but I trusted there was a bigger process at work and I would leave it. Soon the strange notation found a place. The Calgary Stampede mural example is just one of the many short notations I made. The "badge of honor" forgiveness quote discussed in Chapter 4 is an additional example. Another day I was out to lunch with a friend and after I dropped her off, my car flashed a low-fuel message and I knew it had a double meaning. I compared the car's flashing low-fuel message to ego flashing. At other times when I met with family and friends our conversation led to stories that are included in this book or that would trigger a memory or idea.

I found the entire writing process exhilarating. I never wrote with the intention of this becoming a book. I wrote because I felt driven to act on the messages being received; I did not create an outcome. I told people I would write until I was told to stop. If the book were published it would be the will of God because I was fulfilling the role of transcriber. God is the author of this story and many of my life experiences were used to illustrate a point. These are a few examples of the messages I received because the messages were endless, which demonstrates the abundance waiting for us when we are fully open to receiving. May it be so in your life as it is in mine!

Chapter Review:

- Ask God for assistance.
- Faith = Action.
- Look and listen for the answers/signs/messages.

- Act on the answers/signs/messages.
- Accept that everything is as it ought to be.

≈ 10 ≈

Resistance

"Realization"
by Rachael Reimer

Simple words cannot express
just what you mean to me.
For in the time that's come
and gone my heart can finally see.
You cared enough for me
to try to help me on my way,
to put me on the straight
and narrow in hopes I do not stray.
I never knew, for in the past
it seems that I was blind.
I couldn't see the help you gave
and didn't pay you mind.
But now I know for time has passed
and opened up my eyes,
I now can see the truth in things
and see through what were lies.

Sometimes I think my life would make a great TV movie. It even has the part where they say, 'Stand by. We are experiencing temporary difficulties.'"

—Robert Brault, author; www.robertbrault.com

ARE YOU STILL RESISTING THE notion of God or relinquishing your fears and attachments? Meditation is so difficult because it is hard to quiet the mind and experience rest. We are called human beings, but we tend to be "human doings." Is your ego feeling uncomfortable, strange, and out of sorts? Your ego is not used to being silent, and it creates resistance to new concepts. Change is difficult and scary for many. We develop a pattern for being and doing, and the ego will put up a fight because it knows if you relinquish your fears, yearnings, and attachments, it dies. It does not survive when you are cemented in faith. What you resist persists and I encourage you to consider the pain, stress, worry, and suffering you have been going through and give a new way of being and doing a chance.

Penelope, a spiritual leader, told me a story of a man who came to her to be spiritually "fixed." He had just accepted Jesus as his Savior and he could not understand why his life was not magically better. He had searched for answers within his new church family, and when he was unable to get the answers he was looking for, he decided to give Penelope a try. When Penelope met with the man, she soon discovered that he was stuck and he refused to see he needed to take action and to not sit and wait for the telephone to ring like the man wanting to win the lottery. Penelope was not discouraged and she continued to meet with the man to try and assist him with becoming heart-conscious.

One day she enthusiastically discussed the path with him and she believed she was doing a fine job being clear, but he was still stuck; he believed "it"—enlightenment or God's making things clear—would be instantaneous. He rebelled and resisted the notion of "path" or work/faith in progress. A picture from her wall fell directly on the man's head. As he picked it up and turned it over, he saw a photo of a path; it was not one of the photos of Penelope's family or of her vacations, but of a path. He made a joke about the whole thing and left her office.

Penelope rehung the photo and ensured it was secured. The photo had never fallen before. During a follow-up meeting with the man, he resisted the information from the previous meeting, the path was discussed, and once again the photo fell off the wall and landed on his head. He decided that maybe he should pay better attention and stop digging in his heels. This is a prime example of resisting answered prayers, even when the answer had literally banged him on the head. Since God loves us, He is patient and He will persevere to provide the answers to us, even if it sometimes means banging us on the head to get our attention.

God, like any healthy parent, wants to do so much for His children, but we will not let Him. We are rebellious and have temper tantrums; we are determined to make do on our own. On one of the *Country's Family Reunion* DVDs, country-music singer Johnny Russell tells a story about how he would give his concerns to the Lord and then take it back to handle it himself, which resulted in the matter never turning out well. His solution was to get a prayer box. Johnny would write his prayers to the Lord and put them in that sealed wooden box so he could not take his prayers back from the Lord. Once the box was full, he would get another one and continue on. Johnny found the Lord answered his prayers when he stayed out of the way.

When I resigned from my job as a Victim Services practitioner and I was scheduled to meet with my employer for an exit interview, I asked God for support and guidance. When I attended the final meeting with my employer, it seemed like a strange situation. Three months after my initial resignation I had completed the proposal I was writing and the training I was giving; we met for less than five minutes and my employer told me my record of employment and final check would be ready immediately. I asked when he would know whether or not the proposal was successful, he said he had no idea and the meeting seemed to be over. I asked if that was all, and he said, "Yes, there is no need to thank you, is there, because you know we value your work," and the meeting was concluded.

Even after all my efforts on mind-body-spirit connection, I left the meeting feeling like there was a void. I knew God answered my prayers because the meeting was an indicator to me that the proposal would not be successful or I would not be working on it because my time there had come to an end. But I struggled with the whole situation because my previous experience was to remain attached to the outcome of the proposal. My ego was telling me I needed praise at the same time I knew I did not. I did not call my friends and create a grievance story, but at the same time I struggled to completely let go and appreciate that God answered my prayers.

I recalled a conversation with Joan Borysenko, PhD, author of *Fried: Why You Burn Out and How to Revive*, during a lunch break from her workshop. We discussed my work, burnout, and faith. She told me I was no longer in the old, and I was not yet in the new; I was in between. I realized I was currently experiencing the in-between and I was resisting the news God provided. It took me two days to let it go and become comfortable with the answer I received. The entire time I was aware I was fighting my ego and God. I knew deep within my being, God was helping me, but I was giving a herculean effort to keep my old patterns. Once I finally relented and quieted down, I was at peace and remembered peace was preferable to the war I had going on in my mind. Although you may have the best of intentions, you will still resist, but the essential factor is to quiet the mind and recognize ego. Once you obtain some measure of peace you tend to prefer it and will seek it more often, but like all new things it takes practice.

We continue to want a view from God's position. We believe if we have a view from the high place, we will be satisfied, fulfilled, able to release and be settled, but when we cannot be satisfied from our current locale we will not be satisfied from a view on high. If we had a shortcut to obtain the higher view, the ego would want to dominate because it is forever seeking, seeking, seeking—never satisfied. Only when we can accept our current position we might be eligible to achieve a higher view.

When you are pessimistic you find misery, but when you allow your imagination to soar with joy, your mind moves from darkness to light. When you allow misery in your heart you make way for dis-ease.

Chapter Review:

- When you start resisting a new path, meditate or be quiet or still.

- Continue to practice your new skills until they become a natural way of being.

- Make your own prayer box.

☞ 11 ☜

Discernment

"Each one has to find his peace within. And peace to be real must be unaffected by outside circumstances."

—Mohandas Gandhi

Teachers open the door, but you must enter by yourself.

—Chinese proverb

*D*ISCERNMENT; WHAT DOES IT mean? Spiritual discernment is all about judgment of the ego. You can receive messages from many sources and they will be abundant, but you still need to discern whether or not the messages are from God or your ego. Remember the ego is all about justification of yearnings and if it can create an opportunity for a message to appear, it will, but you need to take a second, minute, hour, or several days to judge where the message is coming from. When a drug addict runs into a drug dealer on the street, it can be seen as a sign to buy drugs because the drug addict has a yearning and will create any sort of justification to get his needs met. You have yearnings that are much more socially accepted, like shopping or food, but the craving is the same, as are the justifications you create to get your needs met. The first rule of discernment is *it cannot be harmful to self or others*.

When teenagers are going through those rebellious years and your hair is turning gray from the strain, the entire teenage process is about discernment. For many years your children lived by your rules and beliefs, by school policies, and by society's standards. Teenagers are weighing all of those "forced" rules and policies against what they are discovering for themselves. It is an especially testing time because teenagers, tend to swing from one extreme to another, trying on new thoughts and values like clothes, which is why each day is a new surprise when they come home with purple hair or a tongue piercing or a tattoo.

Although this may be a trying time for you as the parent, if you have been able to create a format for open dialogue with your children and you teach them the art of discernment, you have successfully created a toolbox at their disposal. When you teach children and do not preach, when you are always open to the learnings they provide, a loving environment is created for your home, and it extends out to the universe. It is fantastic when teenagers have the opportunity to discern while in your home because they know it is a safe haven and you will be there to catch them when they stumble and fall. Hmmm . . . sounds a lot like God's love for all human beings.

Questioning messages is vital and God will not get mad. He will be glad. You are not being disloyal; you are being spiritually smart. I encourage you to question all things and look within your heart for the answer that is right for you. Ultimate wisdom is to know the spirit, and it may be opposed to common sense. Noah built an ark on faith. God is about possibilities. When you experience challenges on the road it is an opportunity for discernment; stop and check in. When you are pushing a rock uphill, stop and discern, because life is not meant to be a constant struggle and if you are continuously pushing it may be your ego. Asking questions about life and its meaning leads to pearls of wisdom.

Never judge your choices or discernment on how others respond. Remember Twyla? If she had listened to others, she would still be living in her old community, fighting for child support, and completely miserable. Although her friends and family wanted the best for her, they thought the best was to have a scripted plan. Twyla's decision is an example of ultimate wisdom because it went against common sense. Twyla was able to continue on her path because she felt at peace; she had inner certainty when there was outer confusion or chaos.

When you give yourself a breath, settle your mind, and when you are still and quiet, you are able to reflect on the messages you receive. Indian guru Sai Baba said, "You can hear the footsteps of God when silence reigns in the mind." You will know the message is right when you feel peace. You still may have a few fears creep in, but you can always return to the reassurance of the peaceful feelings, and continue to discern along your path.

God is good; He is all about peace, love, and joy. When you start second-guessing your choices and decisions, please check in with God, because you need the reassurance, which is what signs are all about. God's love is expressed through you when you are happy and peaceful and everyone responds to it. No matter what the activities of the day bring, take time for silence, because understanding follows.

My experiences have been when God speaks, it is in short words or messages, usually not in long paragraphs. Flash thoughts, hunches, intuition, knowing, voices, etc. are all messages from God to stimulate thinking and feeling; you did not just happen upon a book, song, bumper sticker, etc. that had meaning; you were led to it. God wants you to question the whole process because it will eventually lead to further enlightenment.

As you read this book you need to weigh what you are absorbing and look within, because you will know what is right for you. I have discovered each religion has similar core beliefs, like the Ten Commandments, but they differ on the path to spiritual enlightenment. If you have an interest in learning more about the Bible, find a good interpreter's Bible and/or spiritual teacher. The Bible is complicated and should not be taken literally. It helps to have input from other sources and it is valuable to have someone to bounce ideas off of. It is important be discerning about books and teachers because more confusion can be created if you do not have a suitable guide. Remember, God is about love, not fear, and when you sense His presence pass from the book to your mind, your heart you will know you have found the beauty, understanding, and harmony of God's perfect love.

My teenage nephew Joe is enthusiastic about his social-studies class because the teacher allows open communication in the classroom. The teacher believes it is the only way the students will learn. Every thought is more than a thought; it is a nugget for other thoughts: When a student shares an idea or opinion, others are able to give feedback or contribute to the dialogue, creating an opportunity for growth. Opportunities arise for people who can use them, and a lack of opportunity could be the inability to see and use what has been provided. An open mind and heart sees opportunity; you do not walk around with rose-colored glasses on. You still have the ability to recognize danger—it just means you have the clarity to distinguish the difference.

When Joe was in grade six his class started learning about evolution, and when he asked where God fit, he was told they could not discuss God, and the teacher refused to explain why he could not speak of God. Joe came home from school very upset because he could not understand what happened. His mother had to explain the school policy of not being offensive, and why God was taken out of the curriculum. Joe replied that he was offended, and didn't that count?

In grade nine they talked about the impact the church has had on science. Joe pondered the question: when the only focus is science, is *it* not then a religion? Joe has discerned there is a place for science. He believes both science and God are important. Joe realizes science continues to evolve and make adjustments, like Pluto no longer being a planet, and he hopes the same respect can be given for the wonders of God. The willingness to communicate openly creates wisdom while the heart remains youthful.

Joe and I had an ongoing debate about the television show *The Simpsons*. I believed the show was violent and represented what is currently wrong with our society. Joe's perspective was that it is funny and it talks about things other shows or adults often do not talk about, like God. The show has been a part of our culture for over twenty years, and I decided I needed to communicate with Joe with an open heart and mind. My focus had been on the *Itchy and Scratchy* portion of the show, and Joe agrees it is violent. The television adults also believe this portion is violent and have protested it being on, just like we do in the real world. The show pokes fun at everyone equally, and Joe says each week he and his classmates discuss the latest episode. Many times Joe has quoted one-liners and I laugh, and afterwards he tells me it was from *The Simpsons* and I am being hypocritical. He is correct to call me on my mixed messages. When I actually took the time to sit down and to discuss the show with him, I was surprised at how many good messages Joe was receiving, especially pertaining to God. He was able to ask me many thought-provoking questions and then describe how they related to an episode of *The Simpsons*. Joe used discernment to determine *Itchy and Scratchy* was violent, but at the same time he was able to see insights about the show where I wasn't. He told me I was like Lisa Simpson and I now take it as a compliment.

You may think, All I need is the Law of Attraction; who needs God? The law of attraction manifests through your thoughts. If you stay focused on positive things in your life then you will automatically attract it, but if you focus on negativity you will attract it into your life.

The Law of Attraction, like positive affirmations, is an excellent tool, but what is your spirit telling you? When in crisis, the unsteadiness of life apart from God rises and the only way to have stability is through faith in God. All the ideas of paradise lack the quality of genuineness unless they embrace the spirit of God.

Margaret J. Wheatley, author of *Turning to One Another: Simple Conversations to Restore Hope to the Future*, wrote, "Listening is such a simple act. It requires us to be present, and that takes practice, but we don't have to do anything else. We don't have to advise, or coach, or sound wise. We just have to be willing to sit there and listen." Often we do not spend enough time listening to ourselves or others. We are too busy creating activity or wanting to jump into the conversation to share our own thoughts. When you have an opportunity to really listen or be heard, you may be surprised by the outcome. Often the exercise of listening is more challenging for the listener and if you have the temptation to jump in, I encourage you to sit on your hands. When you sit on your hands your mouth remains shut.

I encourage you to get together a group of friends, family, or acquaintances and use the following sharing-circle exercise for discernment. When I facilitated a women's group, we dedicated one afternoon a week to sharing. The groups always sat in a talking-circle format and the rules for sharing during the afternoon sessions were as follows:

A talking-stick was provided. Whenever one person had the stick the other participants could not speak unless the recipient of the stick, asked for input. The purpose was to allow the speakers as much uninterrupted time as needed to share, because as a society it is rare to have an opportunity to just speak. Sometimes when we talk out loud and uninterrupted, we gain great insight. You may feel like you are vomiting words and emotions, and you may experience physical pain as you release what has been held you in your mind-body-spirit.

A box of tissues was placed in the middle of the circle and if the speaker started to cry, she could request a tissue or she could get it herself. This was because often when someone cries, the person observing is uncomfortable, and if tissues are thrust at the speaker, it may stop her from continuing or interrupt her flow. The speaker can interpret the action as an indication that something she said was wrong or that there is something wrong with her.

Hugging was not permitted unless the speaker asked for it. Often hugs are given because the observer needs comforting, not the recipient. Hugs can be interpreted like the tissue, as an indication that there is something wrong with the speaker. Also, many individuals have experienced physical and sexual abuse, and unwanted touching can be quite harmful. It was also important for the recipient to be able to voice needs, like asking for a tissue or a hug, because often people who have been victimized have lost the ability to do so.

After the speaker completes her sharing, the stick moves on to the next person and at that time the new speaker can comment on what she heard. Often the sharing triggers a memory or a feeling for the listeners. If a person receives the stick and does not have anything she wants to share, the stick can be passed on to the next person.

Once the stick makes a complete circle, it is passed again to ensure everyone had an opportunity to share, and it provides an opening for anything left unsaid. The passing continues for as many rounds as needed to give everyone satisfaction.

When I attended a workshop with Joan Borysenko, PhD, coauthor of *Your Soul's Compass*, she reminded me of the circle practice as a tool for discernment. This exercise does not need to be conducted with a group; you can do this one-on-one with a friend or spouse. You can start your meditation with a question you want answered. You can be silent and still and listen for the truth. Allow some time to pass for the answer or discernment to come to you. Once you have asked the question, leave it alone and do not focus on it any further. When the time is right, you will have the verdict you need.

In her book *The Call*, Oriah Mountain Dreamer wrote,

I want to remind us all that the world is listening all the time. How we are ripples out from us into the world and affects others. We have a responsibility—an ability to respond—to the world. Finding our particular way of living this responsibility, of offering who we are to the world, is why we are here. We are called because the world needs us to embody the meaning in our lives. God needs us awake. The world we live in is a cocreation, a manifestation of individual consciousness woven into

a collective dream. How we are with each other as individuals,
as groups, as nations and tribes, is what shapes that dream.

God is not a God of disorder, but of peace. When you feel peace you know you have received the answer from God and you can trust in it. When you begin to doubt your path, remind yourself of the peaceful time, and you once again feel immediate peace.

Chapter Review:

- Question the messages you receive.

- Use a tool to discern your truth.

- Add a talking-stick to your toolbox (the stick could be a feather, rock, or a glitter wand).

☞ 12 ☜

Patience

"Love Itself"
by Em Claire, *EmClairePoet.com*

Please do not regret
all those moments that have brought you
Here.
If you are reading this,
then your perseverance has been answered,
and a Grace is coming.
So for now, hold on loosely to where you are.
And like knots on a rope that mark your reaching,
hand over hand
you will continue to climb—
sometimes through ecstasy,
sometimes through white agony, but
higher
into evermore light.
This same formula over
and over again.
Until that day you find yourself

just a beacon;
only flame.
In a place
where even Love Itself has come undone.

"The two most powerful warriors are patience and time."

—Leo Tolstoy

IT IS NOT A QUESTION of what God has in store for me; the question becomes, How long will it take? We are a society of quick fixes: give me a pill or treatment for what ails, versus treating the cause. When you are depressed medication is often a necessary aid, but counseling is also crucial to explore why you are depressed. If you do not explore the source of the depression and seek new coping strategies, you become dependent on medication there-fore, never treating the source. Technology has created a quick push of a button so we can connect with people all over the world in seconds, but if you push Send too quickly on your computer it can lead to more issues than in the days of thoughtful letter-writing when, if you decided the letter needed to be retrieved you had hours to get it back from the mailbox before the carrier picked it up.

Slow down and feel gratitude as each phase brings you closer to your answered prayer in a concrete form. Notice the lessons and love. It takes time for the seasons to change from spring to summer to autumn to winter, but trust and hold fast to your faith, because God judges time by a different clock. He has a heavenly clock ticking, but like the seasons, transformation eventually occurs. Try focusing on the small day-to-day differences, because that leads to the larger picture. One day the leaves bud, the next they bloom, and that eventually leads to them falling off the tree in anticipation of winter snowflakes. We trust the seasons will change; we may have a vague idea when it will occur, but the calendar is not an exact calculator. Now you must trust God that the answer to your prayer has been set in motion. It just may take a while to see the change in season.

Patience is endurance—believing in possibility, trusting your insights, intuitions, hunches, feelings, instincts, etc., but holding fast until the results arrive. Patience is an outward action of love; therefore, be generous with yourself and others and persevere, knowing that love never disappears.

Here is another piece I wrote when I was in the stages of burnout:

A colleague stops by the office on the way out the door to begin her weekend, and you share your feelings of absolute exhaustion and you receive the usual platitudes. So you give yourself an internal shake and you admit you are looking forward to the weekend because you know that two days off work will make you feel as good as new. You move on, knowing yet again another kindly person just does not get it. But who are you to complain; it seems trivial to desire sleep when you just returned from a motor-vehicle fatality resulting in the death of a child. You chastise yourself for being selfish and you compare your life and the many blessings you have and a wave of guilt washes over you. You beat yourself up some more because it is familiar. You carry on, you suck it up, and you put one foot in front of another and life goes on. You shove your feelings deeper and decide today is not the day to look at what is happening to you. Maybe next week. . . .

Another day, you go online and enter your symptoms and find out that you are (a) burnt out, (b) depressed, or (c) both. It seems burnout fits and you look for the quick fix, but all the suggestions seem to take effort and they do not appear to be too quick. You turn away from the computer feeling exhausted and lost because where do your go from here? Exercise is suggested, but you are too tired to get out of your chair. Sleep is recommended, but you toss and turn all night. Eat healthy, but you are too tired to cook; take-out and junk food are quicker. You berate yourself some more because you know better, and besides, you just read what you needed to do. Maybe you'll try these techniques another day when you have more energy. You booked a massage for later today and maybe that will help you to relax and you will be able to sleep . . . maybe.

You compare war stories and you hear people say, "If you think you are burnt out, wait until you hear my story, and then you will know what burnout really looks like or what types of things you should be burnt out about." The other side of the spectrum is those kindly souls that toss the word burnout around like bubbles in a bath: "I'm so burnt out from making cabbage rolls today and I can't possibly consider making any more until next month." The only reason the cabbage rolls were made in the first place is because they are mouth-watering and the purpose of the comment is to ascertain compliments and allow the person to give an Academy Award–worthy performance while nonchalantly shrugging off the compliments like a prize fighter. That is not burnout. The burnout I am speaking about is gut-wrenching, soul-searching—a bottomless, empty-pit feeling. It's a no-more-water-in-the-bucket scenario, all dried up like a prune. There's nothing left to give and no energy to look for recovery. Sleep is a priority and even it is lost because you toss and turn with images of what is not being accomplished or running through your mind are the many horrific events called your life.

Where do you start? How do you step forward? Do you even want to move? It seems that just remaining still takes a whole lot of energy and you just don't have any to spare. It hurts to think, to move, to feel, to be. But still the world continues to turn and still the world expects/demands answers and participation. People tell you after a good night's sleep or several you will feel like your old self. You laugh internally because you have no energy to provide a real laugh. You think, Maybe if I sleep for six months, then it might work. You start to envy the bears because hibernation seems pretty damn good about now. You think of lying down right now, on the floor of the office, and you drool at the thought of a few precious moments of sleep while the busy office buzzes around you.

It seems we put ourselves into pressure situations just to be in the craziness of pressure. We are being busy to be busy, not because we really need to be. Take for example my mother, who will zoom around the house from one task to another, talking on the cordless phone, whipping cookie dough at mach 1 speed while wiping a spill from the floor with a rag using her foot and mouthing to me to check the mail. Is there really any need for such multitasking, or has it become an *ingrained, socially acceptable norm that being busy means the same as being worthy?*

I worked myself into complete exhaustion for what? I don't think I will get angel wings, and if I do, what use are they when I am dead. I mean, they will have a purpose, but what about my earthly purpose? During this stage of my life I read many books about the best gift is to give to others, but for those folks that give to others for a living, volunteer, or are good Samaritans, when they start to tire, are they less Christ-like? Should they continue to push themselves because it is the Christian thing to do or because giving means more to you than the person that has received? Are we selfish or selfless by saying, No more? The torment we put ourselves through, just to try and find our way through this maze called life.

The constant weighing of questions . . . for those people who are responsible, the weight can become too great. The traits that make them caring, loving, giving people can be the very chains that bind them to situations and people, until they begin to drown. Only they are drowning on the inside, suffering silently because they are not accustomed to using their voice for themselves or have forgotten they have one. As heavy chains slowly pull them under, no one notices or acknowledges the disappearance of that caring, loving individual. They may notice the person is a bit more tired for longer periods of time or the person does not pay as much attention as they once did, but they never voice their concern because their crisis is more important. Their crisis is always taken care of by you, and why should they think otherwise, because you are so strong. The brave few who start to dialogue about burnout are met with wrath and resistance because burnout is

God, Are You Listening?

a dirty word in the helping sector, usually because if the other person takes a moment to look at you, they may start comparing where they are and they do not want to go there. Burnout; the end . . . no more! Then the questions compound. What is next? But the person cannot even comprehend the next step because it is too much of a struggle to get through the now. Burnout is a scary word for a helper. Burnout is like kryptonite to Superman. It conjures up such negativity. It also brings about muscles that are tight and knots like a navy rope. I feel better, so tonight I will sleep. I think I will sleep sound tonight; that's wonderful; I'm back on track. But once again sleep eludes me.

People tell me that I will soon feel like my old self. Do I remember what that was like? Do I want to be my old self again? Who was she; what was she like? I cannot remember the details because I am feeling tired again. Life seems heavy and it is very difficult to make decisions. The literature states burnout is wonderful; you will be more spiritual, and it is the best thing you will ever go through. As usual, it all seems like a cosmic joke. How can I imagine the end when I can barely get through the next few minutes, and now I am to imagine this grand adventure? Intellectually I know that the literature is correct, but how do I get through the now? I am tired again; the answers must wait for another day.

When we cannot see the immediate results of our prayers we may think God has failed. When I wrote this passage, God was there all along. I wanted immediate results, and I did not understand time was like the changing seasons. I could not see the small day-to-day differences because

I was focused on a miraculous recovery. I was being transformed each day, resulting in an amazing spiritual awakening. There are times you will have one fantastic experience after another, the messages are abundant, you have discerned, and life is wonderful. Then it seems quiet and you start to question: God where have you gone? Did I do something wrong? Know heavenly time is manifesting your answered prayer and you are in the midst of a changing season. God sometimes speaks in magnificent signs and at other times He leaves us to the silence of faith. Remember your past incidences of answered prayers and be reassured when the time is right the meaning will be revealed.

Chapter Review:

- Endure.

- Continue to endure.

❧ 13 ❧

Discipline

"Only Here for a Little While"
Performed by Billy Dean; written by Wayland Holyfield
and Richard Leigh

Gonna hold who needs holdin'
Mend what needs mendin'
Walk what needs walkin'
Though it means an extra mile

Pray what needs prayin'
Say what needs sayin'
'Cause we're only here
For a little while

Today I stood singin' songs and sayin', 'Amen'
Saying goodbye to an old friend who seemed so young
He spent his life workin' hard to chase a dollar
Putting off until tomorrow the things he should have done

Made me stop and think, "What's the hurry, why the runnin'?

I don't like what I'm becoming, gonna change my style
Take my time and I take it all for granted"
'Cause we're only here
For a little while

Gonna hold who needs holdin'
Mend what needs mendin'
Walk what needs walkin'
Though it means an extra mile

Pray what needs prayin'
Say what needs sayin'
'Cause we're only here
For a little while

Let me love like I'll never see tomorrow
Treat each day as though it's borrowed
Like it's precious as a child
Whoa, take my hand
Let us reach out to each other
'Cause we're only here
For a little while

Gonna hold who needs holdin'
Mend what needs mendin'
Walk what needs walkin'
Though it means an extra mile

Pray what needs prayin'
Say what needs sayin'

'Cause we're only here
For a little while

Gonna hold who needs holdin'
Mend what needs mendin'
Walk what needs walkin'
Though it means an extra mile

Pray what needs prayin'
Say what needs sayin'
'Cause we're only here
For a little while

"It is not enough to have great qualities; we should also have the management of them."
—François de la Rochefoucauld, writer

WE ARE HERE FOR ONLY a little while; why not make the most of it? We are privileged to be able to carry everything to God in prayer, and when we don't we carry unnecessary pain. Once you are heart-conscious, it is not a guarantee you will remain that way. Your heart can close and you can forget to rely on God and you can carry the pain again, but it gets easier to reopen your heart once you have experienced the wonder.

We started by cleaning the house one room at a time and now it is time to give yourself a moment to appreciate your hard work. But as discussed earlier, the house gets dirty again and cleaning must resume. We are like the house, and we can become lax with our internal cleanup or slow down or stop doing activities that encourage the spirit to glow.

I like to clean the house as I go, by wiping the counters after a spill, cleaning the dishes after eating, and keeping on top of dirty laundry because the chore of cleaning house is not as strenuous when I maintain it. The same can be done for our internal cleaning; if we remain active it is a lot less work in the long run. I find if I go more than three days without prayer or meditation, the old patterns reemerge. The ego is lurking in the shadows, waiting for an opportunity to come out to play. Stay focused on the truth, make healthy changes, and create balance in your life. When we start to have feelings and experiences that are joyous, we often no longer believe we need to continue with the activities that got us to that place. We are healed and fixed, but it is not the case—we are always a work in progress, and it is a good thing, or we would be dead.

When passion begins to wane, and it will because it is our human cycle, it is a dangerous process set in motion. Insights tend to become practices and practices tend to form words and actions expressed with inner conviction. If the process is stopped, the ability to control the mind and to strengthen the spirit diminishes and all is forgotten; you are once again lost. You must be congruent with your inner knowing and outer actions.

A belief in God is not always popular in the modern world, but what is more important: your golden essence or the bleakness that follows you because you are not congruent? Surely the ego will have a tight grip on you if you only display your faith in the confines of your residential home. The good life is eliminated at its foundation if you submit to pressure and you are unable to call your soul your own. When we have inner corrosion it is worse than an outer storm, and when you do not allow your light to always shine you are only half awake.

The door must be opened from within. There is no way to open the door from the outside. You hold the key. When you welcome God, He comes with an abundance of solutions for all sorts of problems, and He satisfies all your needs. If you find the thought of God too much to grasp, look at the situation before you and patiently begin spiritual inquiry. Once you see hardship for what it is, you can understand the offer of spiritual prosperity.

God is with you always, but there will not be constant dialogue because silence promotes insight. You may have a moment of panic and forget He is within you because this is a new experience and mastery takes time. If and when this happens, go to your toolbox to jog your memory. This experience will be added to the list of the many lessons you will learn as you journey through life. My hope is that you can pick up this book and read any chapter and know it leads to a better life—a life with God. This book ends, but my optimism for you is that the learning begins. May the Peace of Christ be with you!

Chapter Review:

- Remain disciplined.

- Check out your toolbox.

- Use a tool to jog your memory about relying on God.

- Add a candle to your toolbox to remind yourself of your essence or glow.

The End and the Beginning

"Amazing Grace"
by John Newton

Amazing grace! How sweet the sound
That saved a wretch like me!
I once was lost, but now am found;
Was blind, but now I see.

'Twas grace that taught my heart to fear,
And grace my fears relieved;
How precious did that grace appear
The hour I first believed.

Through many dangers, toils and snares,
I have already come;
'Tis grace hath brought me safe thus far,
And grace will lead me home.

The Lord has promised good to me,
His word my hope secures;
He will my shield and portion be,
As long as life endures.

Yea, when this flesh and heart shall fail,
And mortal life shall cease,
I shall possess, within the veil,
A life of joy and peace.
The world shall soon dissolve like snow,
The sun refuse to shine;
But God, who called me here below,
Shall be forever mine.

When we've been here ten thousand years,
Bright shining as the sun,
We've no less days to sing God's praise
Than when we'd first begun.

John Newton was born in London July 24, 1725, the son of a commander of a merchant ship that sailed the Mediterranean. When John was eleven, he went to sea with his father. John ultimately became captain of his own ship, in the slave trade. He decided to become a minister. In 1780, as a minister in London, he drew large congregations and influenced many, among them William Wilberforce, who would one day become a leader in the campaign for the abolition of slavery.

AS MENTIONED EARLIER, during a despairing time in my life, I conversed with God by writing. What follows is another communication from God. I remember engaging in this conversation, but I was blind to the message until I began working on this book.

Since the beginning of Biblical times there have been many generations on the journey of discovery for Supreme Consciousness to be like God, the Creator. To obtain supreme consciousness you need to go to your heart, love yourself, and then love the world, and then all things become clear. The battle with evil is not with an outside source or spirit; it is a battle with the mind. We need to control our minds to maintain consciousness. When we allow our mind to be undisciplined, it wanders to the negative past, present, or future. Remaining in the present takes dedication, as does remembering to love thyself and others.

The Bible is a story of the journey to consciousness, not a battle between God and Satan. The Bible story as a whole is an illustration of the mind battling positive and negative thought. Jesus was enlightened and He was born remembering His Highest Consciousness. Like in any good book, the story eventually must come to an end, and Jesus was the surprise party guest that appeared and imparted great wisdom. Many times throughout the Bible the story got stuck and stagnant and Jesus was introduced to rejuvenate the storyline. Although the book ended, the learning continued; thus the Bible became a book of expertise on consciousness. The Bible is not represented in the manner in which it proclaimed. The Bible has deeper meaning in the words it uses and the stories it tells. It does not predict the future and it is not a scientific document about the creation of earth.

When I wrote this, I was in the midst of burnout and I had been reading and rereading the book of Job in the Old

Testament of the Bible. The first time I read Job I believed it would be comforting to be able to read a story of someone else who had suffered for a long time and maybe I could find some comfort in the words. I actually found the story to be quite confusing. Often when I could not sleep I would get out of bed and open my Bible at random and read whatever I was drawn to, and many times it was the book of Job.

When I attended a retreat I discussed my circumstances with a staff member, and I wondered if I needed to leave my job because I was dreaming about the files I worked on over the years. One evening during the retreat we were entertained by children who sang and played musical instruments. Their faces and voices were angelic, but as I listened, images of bodies in the morgue filled my thoughts and I was no longer hearing or seeing the beauty before me. That experience confirmed for me that I was deep into burnout. I would not be able to function much longer at my job, and I was not functioning much better in my personal life. Although I knew the predicament I was in, I was unable to move forward; I was frozen. I had confidence that God would eventually provide and all would end well, but I was concerned about how long the suffering would last. I linked my life to my understanding of Job, which was that he believed in God but suffered through a long period in his life before things got better. I was not sure how much more suffering I could handle, and at the same time knew I could not continue to be in turmoil much longer and be functional.

God provided the answers I sought, but I was blind to the messages because I was too attached to my grievance story and my perception of the spiritual world. When I wrote the words from God, I was unable to discern what was coming from me and what was from God. I was worried someone would think I was mentally ill, and sometimes I wondered that myself. I was afraid others would judge me regarding the passage about the Bible not being a battle between God and Satan, and how I compared Jesus to a character in a storybook. I was afraid to approach anyone to discuss this, including my husband and my trusted spiritual leader. I felt like I was betraying my upbringing and potentially cursing God even though I loved Him. I stopped writing to God after this experience, I was overwhelmed and it was too much for my already-full plate. I took my burdens back to deal with them on my own and I decided the best action was no action and I would wait for a miracle because it was the safest endeavor. I waited and I continued to suffer. But I did get some relief; the retreat leader recommended I discuss a medical leave from work with my family physician. The retreat leader told me that I was capable of returning to the job, but eventually I would be called out to a tragedy and I would stop being able to function, putting myself and others at risk. That scared me because, after all, I was in my profession to help others, not to do harm.

When I returned home, I met with my doctor and counselor, and I took a six-week medical leave. I worked hard during that period on exercise, nutrition, being in nature, listening to music, learning to laugh again, drinking water, attending therapeutic healing sessions, and practicing meditation and deep breathing, and I started sleeping and resting, and I consumed books on spirituality. I meditated often throughout the day and for hours at a time. At the end of the six weeks I was in a healthier place, my mind was quiet, my energy had improved, but I still was far from recovered despite having some amazing spiritual experiences. A gradual return to work plan was arranged with my employer. These methods became my daily practice and I changed my entire lifestyle. I knew if I stopped I would drown. I continued to heal, and I understood why the burnout literature described the act of burning out as a spiritual experience—it was true.

I needed to burn out to give all my burdens, worries, and fears to God, because it was the only way I could become heart-conscious. I continued to learn and have experiences of blessings, love, forgiveness, letting go, and faith, and I received signs. I still struggled and stumbled along the way, especially when I took a break from some of my practices when I resisted and did not discern. I did not go any longer than three days without meditation or prayer before some of the old routine would start to pull me under, and I would hurriedly return to my new system. I became disciplined. My mind-body-spirit was healing and I could see my golden essence or flame shining, but it was not until I took a leap of faith and quit my job that my spirit blazed and soared. I describe my glow as swallowing the sun, and when people comment on how I look, I ask if they can see the light coming from me because I feel like I am shining like a beacon on a lighthouse.

It was not until I started writing this book that my blinders were removed regarding the book of Job. I knew

I needed to include Job in my writing, but I thought it would be referenced in Chapter 4 as part of the discussion of forgiveness in relation to grief. On the drive to pick up my spiritual friend for a lunch date, the passage about Jesus calling out to God on the cross—"My God, my God why have you forsaken me?" [Mark 15:34 (NIV)]—entered my mind, and I knew it fit for the grief discussion. As I shared my miraculous experiences during the writing of this book with my spiritual friend, we discussed Job. I informed her that I found Job to be very confusing, but I was being called to write about him and to share my connection. I was provided with the material I needed and I returned home to begin my study of Job. As I originally thought, the book of Job is difficult to comprehend and is the most misunderstood and misquoted book of the Bible. To my surprise I learned the story was not based on reality, but that instead the book of Job is a poetic book. I had been measuring myself against a fable written by a poet. No wonder I was confused.

Job is a story about a man who lived more than 4,000 years ago and who was honorable and faithful to God and performed the necessary rituals to prove his loyalty and to ensure his protection. Job was healthy and wealthy, with a family and many employees. In modern terms, his wealth could put him into the Fortune 500. Job's suffering started after a conversation between God and Satan.

My belief about Satan is that he is not a horned monster with a pitchfork, nor is he evil. My spiritual friend provided me with some reference material because I struggled to explain my beliefs; the book *The Origin of Satan*, by Elaine Pagels, states "[The] Hebrew storyteller's term for Satan is the angel of challenge, or one who acts as an adversary meant to block or obstruct human activity. The Greek term devil means one who throws something across one's path"; Satan acts on God's behalf to present challenges, obstacles, and blocks to oppose human desires because God is trying to protect us from harm. God's protection of us is just like when a parent blocks a child from touching a hot stove or prevents a teenager from taking the family car to a weekend party where alcohol maybe available. Satan has been sent by God to prevent worse harm. Satan has a purpose just like the angel of death, and both are accepted in God's heavenly kingdom.

My belief about God is that He is a God of love and He would never send his angels to earth to hurt us and perform harmful acts. He would never impose a catastrophe or any type of pain upon His children. God allows famine, war, and disease because each of us has Free Will. We do not want to take responsibility for our behaviors; we need to blame someone—if not God, then Satan. We do not leave old patterns too quickly. There is evil in the world, but it has been at the hand of humans. When we stop harming ourselves, others, and the planet, the world will be a peaceful place. Every earthquake, oil spill, harsh word uttered, and fight is an opportunity to become heart-conscious and accept God.

On an episode of The Simpsons the community informs Marge that Bart was born evil. Marge thinks back to her pregnancy and remembers a time when she attended a ship-launching party and as the champagne bottle broke against the ship a drop of alcohol landed in her mouth; therefore maybe the community was correct—maybe Bart *was* born evil. The show illustrates how silly the community was regarding their belief about Bart being born evil. Babies are not born evil; spiritual awakening must grow and mature.

You may think changing the world is a useless endeavor and it will never be achieved, but the world changes one individual at a time. A ten year-old boy was visiting his grandmother for the weekend, and as they drove down the old country road to her home, she saw a bottle on the side of the road. The grandmother stopped the car and asked her grandson to pick-up the bottle because they would recycle it. As he neared the bottle his grandmother saw that it was broken and she told him to leave it. The boy replied, "This is God's planet and we need to keep it clean and we don't want any animals to get hurt from the broken glass." He got into the car with the broken glass and as they neared her home the grandmother asked the boy who told him about God and keeping the planet clean. He said, "No one told me, it is just what I think." The grandmother was surprised by her grandson's spiritual view. The grandmother retold the story many times about how she recycled because it was the right thing to do, but this was the first time she became conscious regarding the connection between God and the planet. This new level of consciousness made her more appreciative of her surroundings. One word or action can make a difference. One little boy made a difference to the planet and his grandmother.

There has never been more evidence than now regarding our global connection economically, politically, and environmentally, so why would spirituality not also enter into consideration?

When we complain about people in power, like the politicians, we must remind ourselves we are responsible for the authority we have, unfortunately, misplaced. If we want change then we must demand it. Politicians will do the bidding of the people, and you only need to consult a Gallup poll to see how guided they are by it. We become too complacent and apathetic after elections. We tell ourselves it is just how the world of politics works and that politicians are all corrupt. It is up to us to demand something different, to seek accountability. You do not need to be a prisoner of your environment; many have changed the world around them; think of Moses, Nellie McClung (a women's-suffrage advocate), Abraham Lincoln, Mohandas Gandhi, Rev. Dr. Martin Luther King, Jr., and Rosa Parks. Before all of these individuals began their journey of assistance they did not know the profound impact they would have on the world.

The Book of Job describes Satan and God chatting about whether or not Job would remain a faithful follower of God if he were not prosperous and basically lost everything that was dear to him. God allowed Job's faith to be tested, but Satan was told that Job could not be killed. If a dialogue like this did take place between God and Satan, it is like two friends getting together over coffee and discussing a mutual friend's or a family member's belief system. Even if they wondered about the person's true beliefs, they would not wish harm to the person or hope that one disaster after another would be orchestrated to test the person.

According to the story, Job's suffering started after this dialogue, and the first losses are his oxen and donkeys, and his servants are put to the sword. Job withstands the onslaught and remains faithful to God, and once again Satan wants to put Job to the test, as the story goes. God allows for another experiment, but Satan is told he cannot kill Job.

The second bout of suffering is fire falling from the sky; it burns all the sheep and servants. Still Job remains faithful and once again more suffering is allowed. This time he loses his camels to raiders and again his servants are put to the sword. Once more, Job remains faithful, and again more suffering is allowed. The next tragedy is a mighty wind that strikes the house where Job's sons and daughters are feasting, and they all die. Job remains faithful, so now Satan asks God to allow him to touch Job's skin because "A man will give his all for his own life" [Job 2:4 (NIV)]. Satan is allowed to touch Job's skin, but he is not allowed to kill him. Job now suffers sores all over his body, and his wife asks Job if he is going to curse God now, but he remains faithful.

Job has three friends who come to visit because they are concerned about him and all of the disasters that have befallen upon him. Job remains silent or refuses to talk for a very long time. When Job speaks he calls out to God in frustration, wanting to know why this is happening to him because he has been a "Good follower of His ways." God is silent. The friends, however, begin to impart their wisdom.

They want Job to admit he was at fault, he did something wrong, he sinned against God and is being punished. One friend is a theologian and passes considerable knowledge on to Job about his wrongs against God and the need for redemption. This type of "support" is like when someone tells you, "You made your bed and now you'd better lie in it" or pats your head and says "There, there" in a patronizing voice or uses platitudes or takes an annoying know-it-all, holier-than-thou stance. Still Job remains faithful and firm that he did not betray God.

After this exchange God asks Job if he understands the way of the universe. God is asking Job if he has Ultimate Wisdom and if he is heart-conscious. At that moment Job realizes he is not. Job performs the rituals of faith—he has understood intellectually, but not with his heart. Job's mind and heart got caught up in the obsession of rituals of faith; he did not realize the suffering was weaning him from his old way of embracing God until he came face-to-face with God. Job was then able to rid himself of too much self and allow his heart to really see. Many of us are like Job; we go to church, we understand and follow the Ten Commandants, we are morally upright, and we obey the rules and laws of our country, but we are missing the crucial element, which is heart-consciousness.

The Book of Job ends with God speaking to Job's friends and informing them He is not pleased and they must sacrifice a burnt offering to Job. (Animal sacrifices were explained to me from the perspective of an African custom, and it means that an animal is killed for food and is offered as a meal in celebration.) Job becomes more prosperous after this experience, with many animals and the most beautiful children in the land. Job lives to be 140 years old and is able to interact with four generations. He dies old and joyous.

Job experienced many challenges, and each was an opportunity to give himself fully to God. Throughout the journey, Job still had Free Will. Isn't it wonderful to think that challenges, blocks, and unfulfilled desires are times that God is keeping us from harm through the work of His angel Satan? Only when Job relinquished his belief system or changed the CD or took his mind off autopilot about his definition of faith was he awakened. He once again prospered, but this time it was not about material possessions or having formalized spiritual practices because it was the correct thing to do. Job was all about spiritual fulfillment and he remained heart-conscious until his death.

The Book of Job could easily be called "Elizabeth Hutchinson's Memoirs." Job's journey is my story, and I needed to lose everything to gain everything. The burnout stage of my life was the "test." In the midst of exhaustion and the complete feeling of aloneness, I called out to God in despair, asking, "What have I done to deserve this?" but at the same time I knew I had done nothing wrong. I was ritualistic with my faith; I prayed, I attended church, followed the Ten Commandments, I obeyed the rules and laws of my country, I was compassionate, I helped others for my career, and I volunteered hours of service to others. Some of my friends, family, and coworkers had the best of intentions, but provided clichés of wisdom. I, like Job, was missing the message and even when God told me directly, I still missed it. I had become so corroded from the busyness and the treadmill of life, I could not see my golden essence, my flame, my spirit. I was searching for God, but He was right there within me all along. I was blind and could not see, and I was looking in the cupboard with eyes of poverty. All I needed to do was take one easy step to free myself from what was holding me back. Once I relinquished my fears and attachments, I found an all-encompassing love so vast it is beyond imagination—the enormity of the universe.

This is the continuation of the dialogue I presented at the start of this chapter:

Jesus like Buddha, Rev. Martin Luther King Jr., Mother Teresa, Mohandas Gandhi, and Nelson Mandela, are all enlightened beings working at a high level of consciousness. What separates Jesus from the others is we were told before His birth that He would remain aware of His consciousness. Jesus informed us throughout His life what to expect and how to maintain consciousness. Jesus also informed us of His death and what was to follow. Jesus was the perfect human and the perfect example of the highest level of consciousness. The others forgot consciousness at birth, like all of us, but they were able to rediscover consciousness much faster than most. The question now becomes, How do I maintain my level of consciousness?

A portion of this passage was written on letterhead titled, *The Power of Conscious Leadership*, from the book *Who You Are Is How You Lead: How the Power of Conscious*

Leadership Can Shape the Leader You Want to Be, by Gail Gibson. But I was blind.

When you become heart-conscious it is not a guarantee that you will remain receptive. Life still presents challenges; you have Free Will and you will forget again. There are times you will feel irritated, negative, and grumpy, and when this happens it is an opportunity to be still and take inventory. The way to maintain heart-consciousness is to use the tools in your toolbox to keep your mind-body-spirit balanced. At times the mind can feel like the enemy, but it is not; it is the tool for Free Will. It is up to you to determine what you want your outcome to look like. When you are conscious mind-body-spirit, with love as your primary focus in life, you use Free Will to create your earthly life in a manner that is loving to yourself and the world. Free Will is one of God's greatest gifts to us! A heart-conscious person uses Free Will to love self—to express love to the world. Life has no beginning and no end because the "end" is the beginning of a higher level of consciousness.

When I approached the end of writing this book, I had a dream about an Aboriginal chief who came to visit me. The chief said, "It is the white man's way, not the Indian way." I started to rise and he told me to continue to lie down. The chief spoke to someone near me and he said, "She is protected and safe," and then he left. When I woke I tried to understand the dream and I had a book called *Bad Medicine*, by John Reilly, and I thought I was meant to read it. As I read, I realized that although the book was excellent it was not the meaning. I started searching my brain for Aboriginal meanings and the thought of an eagle flashed by. I had been reading the book of Revelation in the New Testament of the Bible, and when I picked it up again shortly thereafter, I read about eagles. Eagles are messengers of God. In Aboriginal culture eagles are spiritual protection; they carry prayers, and they bring strength, courage, wisdom, illumination of spirit, healing creation, and a knowledge of magic. The eagle has an ability to see hidden spiritual truths, rising above the material to see the spiritual. The eagle has an ability to see overall patterns and connections to spirit guides and teachings. The eagle also represents great power, balance, and dignity with grace, a connection to higher truths, intuition, and creative spirit—grace achieved through knowledge and hard work. I felt certain the eagle was the message because the entire book has been about mind-body-spirit messages. My journey through burnout and the writing of this book has been a true revelation to me. I am confident that I'm firmly planted on the road to truth and I hope you are too.

Epilogue

"It Only Takes a Spark"
(Pass It On)
by Kurt Kaiser

It only takes a spark to get a fire going,
and soon all those around can warm up in its glowing:
that's how it is with God's love, once you've experienced it:
you spread God's love to everyone, you want to pass it on.

What a wondrous time is spring when all the trees are budding,
the birds begin to sing, the flowers start their blooming;
that's how it is with God's love, once you've experienced it:
you want to sing, it's fresh like spring, you want to pass it on.

I wish for you, my friend, this happiness that I've found—
on God you can depend, it matters not where you're bound;
I'll shout it from the mountaintop; I want my world to know:
the Lord of love has come to me,
I want to pass it on.

"A light is gleaming, spreading its arms throughout the night, living in the light. Come share its gladness, God's radiant love is burning bright, living in the light."

—From: *Greatest of These* CD by Linnea Good

I WOULD LIKE TO CONCLUDE with some personal reflections; this whole book has actually been a reflection and personal experience.

I finally understand the meaning of *Born Again*, a term often used in Christianity to describe a person who has accepted Jesus as their Savior. When I became heart-conscious I saw the world in a new light. It was like I was an infant discovering the world for the very first time. At one time if I even happened to notice an insect, I usually trampled it, but now insects are absolutely fascinating to me. I will often get on the ground like a child and observe what the bugs are doing, and I am in awe of their industriousness. I see the flowers and the trees now. My husband told me he used to say, "look at that beautiful sunset," I would look up for an instant and say, "Yes," and return to whatever I was doing, never really seeing. Now if he says look at the sunset or the moon, I leap out of my chair and spend some time beholding the wonder. I am awake! I now really love and care for others, including strangers. I do my best to make a point of acknowledging the people around me and being fully present while they speak. When someone I encounter rubs me the wrong way, I send love, not discord.

Am I perfect? Absolutely not! I am just beginning to walk, I stumble and sometimes fall, but I know God is there with me every step of the way and He will catch me. I have not developed a new idea or concept. This book is just my take on things and is presented to the best of my ability. I transcribed the messages I received from God. My deepest longing is to communicate what I have learned from God, which leads to enlightenment for others and eventually an enlightened world. I was gifted with new insight—with a need to write and share my findings.

Often we set high ideals for those we care about, and we even do it for movie, music, and sports stars. We have television shows looking for American Idols. When one of our movie, music, or sports idols falls off the pedestal, we are quick to crucify him and the media runs stories nonstop until another fallen idol hits the ground. Where is the love and compassion? The person we once helped elevate we now watch with fasciation at they meet their destruction. The idol often gets caught up in his own hype and as a result falls into a destructive cycle of self-abuse. His prayers for success and fame were answered, but he has forgotten to fill himself with the essential ingredient, which is love. What I caution against is the aspiration to seek perfection in yourself and others. When we have an expectation of perfection from self and others we will be met with disappointment. There was only one perfect human being: Jesus.

We will all die; it is unavoidable. It is the cycle of life, but it is vital to enjoy living now! I have been writing in partnership with God. Sometimes He took the lead or load when it was too heavy for me to bear or understand. Are you awake now? Jesus knew the road map and He had a built-in GPS. We travel an unknown road, but know calling on God is like pushing our car's OnStar button for help.

What makes your heart sing? When we become heart-conscious, our songs change. Check what is playing in your heart. Nothing confronts bullies like hearing the songs of the oppressed. Rev. Dr. Martin Luther King, Jr. and the Freedom March are a prime example. As the marchers walked they sang heavenly songs. When they were arrested and put in jail they used their voices to sing God's praises. The guards could take everything from them except their spirit, which thrived in song. When you have heavenly music playing in your heart, your inner expression becomes an outward display of strength. When difficult and tragic days appear, the music remains. I once was lost, but now am found. It took only a spark to set my heart ablaze; now I am warm from the glow and I pass it on wherever I go. My heart is afire with the glory and messages of God.

Hallelujah!

Celebrate the creation of you!

Be gentle with yourself and know that you will still have some "bad" days. You will snap at your spouse or your children or have limited patience with the sales clerk or you may feel lonely. Old patterns are difficult to break, but the more you persist the easier it becomes. Now when I find myself snapping at my husband I am quick to notice and I change my behavior. Some days just seem not to be going as well as I had imagined, but then I realize I am trying to control the situation. As soon as I give it over to God, I find instant peace. Being disciplined is not easy, but I prefer the results I get with God versus the messes I tend to create.

One day I flew to Chicago for a conference, and the airport was very busy. As I waited for a taxi it reminded me of the television show *The Amazing Race*. There were cars and people everywhere. When I got to my hotel room I was exhausted, hungry, and lonely. I started questioning why I had come, especially without my husband. I realized I had gotten quite used to sharing my travels with him. The only restaurant nearby was Greek and I was not accustomed to eating Greek food, but I trudged into the restaurant anyway. As I sat down at the table by myself, I looked around at all the happy families and couples, and felt very alone. A young man approached my table to fill my water glass and I happened to notice his nametag, which was unusual for me because I am not usually that observant. I was startled when I read his name—it was Jesus. As his name was sinking in I started to look around the restaurant and my spirits lifted and I started to smile. Of course I was not alone—we are never alone. God is always with us, but I had forgotten *again*. I thought it was quite profound that Jesus was serving water to the isolated woman in a Greek restaurant. **The water** symbolizes God's loving gift of the spirit, and when Jesus poured water into my glass, it represented my access to God's gift. Just as in so many Bible stories, Jesus reached out to someone who felt like an "outcast." The Greek restaurant signified Jesus's connection to the Gentiles (Greek term meaning Nations).

The conference was fabulous, and I have been on an amazing race ever since. Each day is a new adventure, but this experience was a good reminder to me. I never saw Jesus again at the restaurant. I thought about asking the staff if they had an employee named Jesus, but I preferred to leave it a mystery. The moment was very special to me and I did not need concrete evidence of his existence. I felt confident that God had sent me a message, and whether or not it was a water boy by the name of Jesus or Jesus from the Bible, I was delighted with the message. Trusting in the mystery is faith in God, and that is all that I need.

I would like to share how writing this book came about. One night I watched the *Country Family Reunion DVD Series* (*www.cfrvideos.com*). Bill Anderson spoke about the song-writing process and he stated that often he begins a song with the title and repeats that title in the last line of the song. I enjoyed hearing the stories and music and I went to bed as per usual. During the night I heard myself saying, "God, are you listening?" The most gentle, loving, caring, and warm voice replied, "Yes, child; are you?" I woke with those words, and with a tremendous feeling of love, I knew that I must get up and write them down. I knew it was a very spiritual moment. I wrote the words on a slip of paper, went to the bathroom, and returned to bed and fell asleep.

In the morning I opened my laptop and wrote the words *God, Are You Listening?* on one page, and on another page I added, "Yes, child; are you?" I started to write, and words poured onto the page. I immediately had an outline of other topics I wanted to write about. I got lost in time and I was surprised to see my husband home eight hours later. I had been writing the entire time, only taking bathroom and refreshment breaks. I continued to write every day. Often I would wake in the middle of the night and scurry out of bed to record my thoughts. Sometimes I wrote pages, and at other times I made brief notes. When driving my car, I often needed to pull off to the side of the road because the words were coming so fast I could not keep up and I knew I must record them or risk losing the message.

When I was writing I had no idea that it would be for a book and I did not think of it as being something that would be published. I wrote because I was called to write. I sometimes thought it might just be a therapeutic process, and at other times I considered it a curriculum. When it was completed, I knew it was a book.

I gave the manuscript to a friend to edit, and then in mid-September 2011, I told her that I really felt that the manuscript needed to be sent to a publisher as soon as possible. I sent the manuscript via email and received confirmation on a Saturday that it had been received. I'd had no expectation about hearing from anyone that soon, and especially not on a Saturday. I was informed that the review process might take months because hundreds of manuscripts are received each week. Shortly after I sent the email to the publishing company I read how some rejections from larger publishing companies actually allowed smaller companies to benefit. I smiled as I read the passage because I just knew.

By October 3, 2011, I had a rejection letter by email from the publishing company, but I did not feel one moment of disappointment. That was on a Monday, and the next day I received another email from a smaller publishing company willing to publish the book. July 4, 2011—Independence Day in the United States of America—I started to write, and in five weeks I had a completed book, but the best news is that I continue to have amazing experiences. When God whispers to us, our lives are changed.

For many years I heard that the Bible was the most beautiful book ever written, but I could never understand the statement. I never let my true thoughts be known because I was taught that I needed to respect the Bible. But I think I feared it more, because when I was in my burnout stage I stopped writing to God because I thought I was attacking the Bible when I questioned some stories from it. Now that I have actually taken the time to explore the Bible and understand when stories are not literal, I too agree that it is a beautiful book. It is a love story about God's relationship with us and our relationships with each other and the planet. The Bible is a wonderful tool for self-discovery.

I encourage you to find a spiritual group that works for you. When you become heart-conscious you want to shout out to the world and engage in discussions with others about your experiences and you want your transformation to continue. You become invigorated by others and having a spiritual group, whether it is on Facebook, on Twitter, in a church, in the park, in a home, or in a chat room, will help you remain heart-conscious. Find a way to reach beyond yourself or the building you meet in, and reach out to the community because everyone's spirit is waiting to shine. You may be able to help others remove some corrosion from their lives.

I encourage you to go out and promote social justice and demand that your government govern with a compassionate heart. Remember while making your demands you must also role-model nonviolence. To govern like a real king would be to govern with love and compassion for humanity. Demand from the government a balance between commerce and people. Demand that they meet people and listen to what the needs of the people are versus telling the people what they need. Generate creative solutions and then act on those solutions. When you invest in people, your home, community, country, and world thank you because you are a champion of the best of humanity.

I also encourage you to be passionate about the planet, not just because it is essential for our survival, but because you appreciate it as a gift from God that needs to be treated with respect. We can have some modern conveniences without destroying ourselves and the planet in the process. Hold in your mind-body-spirit a vision of the world healed and returned to its natural splendor as God intended it to be.

One of my nieces informed me that her one-year-old daughter's first word was *dog*, but she called everything a dog. A cow was a dog, the house was a dog, and the children next door were dogs. I explained that it was not unusual; other children in the family started talking in the same manner and I have heard many similar stories from other parents. It was at that precise moment as I talked on the cell phone while parked on the Dog Creek Road that I had an epiphany—*dog* spelled backwards is *God.*

What if the words were being mangled and the children actually mean God? After all, a dog is man's best friend and no, I do not mean that I think God is a dog. I mean that God is always with us just like a best friend. God, like our best friend, may encourage us to seek better or more for ourselves, but not in a judgmental manner. God, like our best friend, provides unconditional love. When a child sees a cow, house, other children etc., he might exclaim with excitement *dog* because he sees *God* everywhere and in everything. What a blessed way to view the world!

Invite God in to shift things within you and allow Him to work with you. And when you ask God, "Are you listening?" know that his loving response will be "Yes, child; are you?" Jesus fed 5,000 people with fish and bread, and my hope is that this book nourishes you. Praise be to God!

Journal Pages

Journal pages have been provided because it is helpful to record your observations and use this as an opportunity for reflection.

_____

_____

_____

_____

_____

_____

_____

_____

_____

_____

_____

_____

∼

∾

～

Permissions

Appreciative acknowledgments are made to the following authors and publishers who allowed me to reprint the brilliant inspirational quotes or passages from their books and online publications.

"I want to remind us all that the world is listening, all the time." From *The Call*, by Oriah Mountain Dreamer. Published by HarperOne, San Francisco. 2003. All rights reserved. Printed with permission of the author. *www.oriah.org.*

"Love Itself" ©Em Claire. All rights reserved. Printed with permission from the author. *www.EmClairePort.com.*

"Lord, we thank you for the bounty we're about to receive." (awhn 367). Printed with permission from *www.CartoonStock.com.*

"If you want to know the secret of good health, set up home in your own body, and start loving yourself when there." From *Simply Well*, by John W. Travis, MD, and Regina Sara Ryan. Ten Speed Press, Berkeley. 2001. Printed with permission.

"Sometimes I think my life would make a great TV movie. It even has the part where they say, 'Stand by. We are experiencing temporary difficulties.'" Robert Brault. Printed with the permission of the author. *www.robert-brault.com.*

"Thank you for waking me up today." From *My Stroke of Insight: A Brain Scientist's Personal Journey*, by Jill Bolte Taylor, PhD. Viking; published by the Penguin Group, New York, 2008. Printed with permission from the author.

Turning to One Another: Simple Conversations to Restore Hope to the Future, by Margaret J. Wheatley. Berett-Koehler Publishers, San Francisco, 2002. Second edition, 2009. Printed with permission from the author.

"Faith, While Trees Are Still in Blossom." Fred Kaan. Hope Publishing Company, Carol Stream, IL, 1976. All rights reserved. Used by permission. Printed under license #76370.

"A Candle is Burning," by Sandra Dean. Ottawa, Ontario, 1986. Printed with permission from the writer.

"It was my secretary's fault. She forgot to put breathing on my to-do list." Glasbergen Cartoon Service, Sherburne, NY. Printed with permission from the cartoonist. *www.glasbergen.com.*

"Let us be willing to release old hurts." Martha Smock. Printed with permission from the Publisher Unity School of Christianity. Fear Not: Messages of Assurance, Unity School of Christianity, Unity Village, MO, 1986.

"The body needs material food every day. The soul needs spiritual food"; "All techniques and methods of inner development have a common goal. They all aim toward freedom and enlightenment"; "Plant the seed of meditation and reap the fruit of peace of mind." Remez

Sasson. Printed with permission from the author. *www.SuccessConsciousness.com.*

The Hidden Messages in Water, by Dr. Masaru Emoto. Beyond Words Publishing, Hillsboro, OR, 2004. Printed with permission from the author.

"Even though we represent many different First Nations cultures and traditions, we all agree on one basic teaching." *Bridge Between Nations—A History of First Nations in the Fraser River Basin.* Assembly of First Nations, 1993. Printed with permission from the Fraser Basin Council.

Michael J. Tamura gave permission for his quote to be printed.

"Realization," by Rachael Reimer, Quesnel, British Columbia, 2005. Printed with permission from the poet.

"When we rent too much space to disappointment we create a grievance story." From *Forgive for Good: A Proven Prescription for Health and Happiness* by Dr. Fred Luskin. HarperCollins, New York, NY, 2003. Printed with permission from the author.

"Give it Away" © 2006 Sony/ATV Music Publishing LLC, Mr. Bubba Music, EMI Music Inc. and Publisher(s) Unknown. All rights on behalf of Sony/ATV Music Publishing LLC and Mr. Bubba Music administered by Sony/ATV Music Publishing LLC, 8 Music Square West, Nashville, TN 37203. All rights reserved. Used by permission.

Country Family Reunion DVD Series; www.cfrvideos.com. Permission granted by Loren Black President/CEO. *www.gabrielcommunications.com.*

About the Author

Elizabeth Dillman-Hutchinson was born in Truro, Nova Scotia, Canada and lived there until the age of twenty. She moved west to Alberta and then in 1994, moved to Williams Lake, British Columbia where she has remained for over twenty years. She is very happily married with a supportive family including many nieces and nephews. Elizabeth worked in the social sector for eighteen years as a Life Skills Coach, Employment Counselor and Victim Services Practitioner. She is a member of the Canadian Alliance of Life Skill Coaches and she is currently working on her degree in Holistic Theology at AIHT. Elizabeth enjoys scrapbooking, being with family and RV'ing. You can visit her at *www.godandelizabeth.com.*